Emigrate To New Zealand

Avalon's Guide

Emigrate To New Zealand
How To Live The Dream
Without Breaking
The Piggy Bank

www.avalonsguide.com

Helen Winterbottom

www.avalonsguide.com

Copyright ©Helen Winterbottom, 2008

All rights reserved
The moral right of the author has been asserted

ISBN 978-1-877513-00-8

Printed in Wellington, New Zealand
by First Edition Ltd
www.FirstEditionPublishers.com
www.nzbookshop.co.nz

All rights reserved. No part of this publication may be reproduced, stored in a retrieval system or transmitted in any form by any means electronic, mechanical, photocopying, recording or otherwise, without prior permission from the publisher.

Dedication

To Alan, for deciding that New Zealand was the place to take me on our Honeymoon.

To my family – for teaching me that anything is possible, and for being the sort of family that didn't think I was completely bonkers for wanting to move half way round the world.

To all the members (past, present and future) of the EmigrateNZ forum, for having the guts to dream big.

Acknowledgments

I'm sure you all know that books don't get written by just one person. This one is no exception – I just couldn't have done it without:

Douglas and the ENZ forum: the whole reason this book exists is because of them and their willingness to let me prattle on about money and finances.

Cheri and Dave, who called me the "Fairy Dollar Mother" and let me prove that I really did know what I was going on about. Thank you for being brave enough to let me rifle through your accounts, and for continuing to be friends with me afterwards.

Smiler, who helped me turn the original posts into one long thread, and helped me drink a phenomenal amount of coffee.

To Trev and Steve, my mentors – who taught me that mentors are the best way to help you get where you want to go, by following in their footsteps and learning from their mistakes, and who showed me that I could help others learn from my mistakes.

To the CBD group – for their honest appraisal of my original title ideas – you helped me finish. (And it's still not the BNZ pig!)

Alan, my Parents and Brother for not thinking I was an idiot to try writing a book. And for all telling me to get on with the damn thing already!

To everyone who said – "you should write a book!" Cheers!

Contents

A Long Time Ago In A Country Far, Far Away	9
THE BASICS – SHOULD I STAY OR SHOULD I GO?	13
Will I be worse off in New Zealand?	14
Is it cheaper to live in New Zealand?	16
What about the dreaded taxes?	24
Will I have to take a lower wage in New Zealand?	32
Can I negotiate my salary?	36
BUDGETS – THE CUDDLY WAY	39
So, how do I start budgeting? (Arghhhhh)	40
A sample budget.	50
Am I a big spender?	55
How do I keep track of my money?	60
Do I have to grow my own veggies?	68
What about banks and bank charges?	71
Tree hugging and the concept of money.	77
DEBTS- HOW TO DEAL WITH THEM AND GET THEM FROM AROUND YOUR NECK	83
Debts – do I pay them or leave them behind?	85
Getting rid of debt in a nutshell.	90
MORTGAGES IN NEW ZEALAND	99
Can I get a decent, affordable mortgage?	101
Should I pay off my home loan as fast as possible?	107
Should I keep money in the UK or have a smaller mortgage in New Zealand?	111
What on earth is a Revolving Credit mortgage?	115
How do I actually pay off a Revolving Credit mortgage?	121
What Balance do I need in this Revolving Credit account?	125

BUYING YOUR NEW ZEALAND HOME	127
Is it really much easier to buy a house in New Zealand?	128
What's all this BBO & BEO nonsense on house adverts?	138
How do I find out how much to pay for a house?	143
WHAT ABOUT OUR FUTURE FINANCES?	147
How do I save and invest enough to retire on?	149
So I've saved the money, how do I know what to invest in?	151
Pensions, shares or property?	154
Can't I just put my money in the bank and let it grow?	164
What is Kiwisaver?	170
LAQ whats?	185
Heads or Tails – the New Zealand economy for numpties!	191
MAKING THE MOVE – GETTING YOUR BUTT (AND MONEY) TO NEW ZEALAND	198
Can I open a New Zealand bank account before I leave?	199
How do I run my UK bank accounts from New Zealand?	204
How do I move all my £ to my new country?	207
Should I work with $ or £?	216
I'm leaving the UK, is my pension coming with me?	219
So what happens to our UK state pensions?	226
What should we do with UK policies and insurances?	229
When should I apply for my New Zealand Tax Number?	234
Don't I get a tax exemption for four years?	237
Will we get Working For Families Tax Credits?	240
How much does it actually cost to emigrate?	244
How on earth do we get started?	253
Recommended Books and Websites.	258

A LONG TIME AGO IN A COUNTRY FAR, FAR AWAY.....

I was sitting in a rented Motorhome overlooking Takapuna Beach with my husband Alan, my parents and my brother. We were on a "look-see" trip, deciding whether upping sticks to New Zealand was really what we wanted to do. Alan and I had already been to New Zealand the year before on our Honeymoon. As often happens to people that come here; we fell in love with the place, and by the end of our first week, we figured it was worth trying to emigrate. The rest of my family had decided "why not?" when we asked if they would consider coming here as well.

That day on the beach, I had just finished reading a book we had found in Auckland, about paying off your mortgage quickly. I announced to the family at large, that as soon as we got back home, I was going to do a budget and get Alan and myself out of debt. My mum collapsed on the floor laughing. 😁

When she could breath again, and I got over the massive insult, she told me she had always been surprised that I had ever got into financial difficulty in the first place. Or as it happened – the second place as well 😳. You see – in my first year at University (long ago enough that I still got a grant), I came back home with money left over. Now on my second marriage – I was in debt for the second time. We had a largish mortgage (£140,000), but as well as that, we had £14,000 in credit card debt and overdrafts. And we weren't paying it off.

Reading that book, (How to Pay Off Your Mortgage In Five Years by Anita Bell) and taking control of our financial mess, was the start of a very strange journey. By the time we entered New Zealand 13 months later, with our gleaming blue Visa stickers and were "Welcomed Home" by immigration at Auckland airport, we had paid off that £14,000 debt. We started our new life in New Zealand with a clean slate, money in the bank from saving and selling the house and most importantly, new money skills that helped us cope with the financial aspects of life in a new country.

So why on earth would I write a book about money and emigrating to New Zealand? Well, because frankly – it's one area where too many people face problems with their new life, and too many people go home because of it. Let's face it – you decide you want out of the rat race – you want greener pastures; peace and quite; heavenly beaches; a nice cheap house with an acre or two to grow veggies and keep chooks on; and only four-and-a-bit million other people to share it all with. Who cares about the money? That's not what you are moving half way round the world for. Is it?

Well, there's lots of information about how to emigrate out there: how to get your visas; how to ship your worldly goods halfway across the world; a whole host of stuff. But where was the information on how to deal with a new banking system; new and different mortgages; lower wages? And if you found it – what language was it written in? Because it sure didn't sound much like English to me. 😕

Well, hopefully, after reading this (in friendly English – not gibberish 😉) you will know what to expect, and be prepared. Then – you **won't** have to worry about the money, and can get on with the important things in life, like bumming on the beach all day, and enjoying your new life in New Zealand. Because this really is an amazing place to live and I want everyone to have the best chance ever of staying here a long time.

This book exists because of questions that are frequently asked on Emigration forums on the Internet. It started its life as answers to some of those questions on the Emigratenz forum at www.emigratenz.org. It has grown a wee bit since then – but I hope it helps make your journey to a new life here in New Zealand that little bit easier.

The problem with a book that relies on tax policy, immigration rules, and interest rates – is that they change so often. So visit www.avalonsguide.com to see what changes are occurring and any news that I think migrants could do with knowing about finances. Otherwise I'm going to have to rewrite this every six months, and that would seriously dent my time on the beach.

I need to make a disclaimer (just in case). I am not a financial advisor or money "expert". I have absolutely **no** qualifications in anything financial, or even vaguely resembling economics, not even an NCEA! While I'm at it, I'm not a lawyer either. I have a calculator, my brain, a record of where my money is coming from and going to, and I made time to learn how money works. (Lots of that was taken up deciphering the gibberish into English☺) It's really not rocket science – it just looks that way at first.

Everything in here I've read in books, papers or is my personal experience over the last few years, both as a new migrant to New Zealand and before that back in the UK. It's all learned the hard way but it's all my own opinion and should be taken as such – sometimes a sense of humour (and a Flat White) will also help. (You will soon find that I believe that everything looks better with a good cup of New Zealand coffee.)

THE BASICS – SHOULD I STAY OR SHOULD I GO?

"I may not have gone where I intended to go, but I think I have ended up where I intended to be."
Douglas Adams

Making the decision to emigrate anywhere is huge. Sometimes it's so huge, we don't even really understand just what a honking decision we have made until after we have made it, and we are sat in our new home.

At which point, we may suddenly realise all the things we wish we had thought of before we left.

So here are what I consider to be the very first things I wish we had thought of and realised, before we moved!

WILL I BE WORSE OFF IN NEW ZEALAND?

> *"They say it is better to be poor and happy than rich and miserable, but how about a compromise like moderately rich and just moody?"*
> Princess Diana

Without a doubt, a lot of people are.

But it's certainly not written in stone that you have to be financially worse off here than you were back home. We are actually a lot better off financially here in New Zealand than we were in the UK. So it is possible, although for my money (excuse the pun) you probably have to "think outside the box" most of the time to make the numbers work. We have done this with a mix of watching what we spend so it's less than we earn, saving to invest and most importantly, getting educated. Educated about how exactly to budget, invest and how to use the money to our advantage rather than the banks.

One of the many things (on top of the space, beaches and general wonderfulness of the place) that attracted us to New Zealand was what we saw as the lower taxes and the ability to accumulate assets without being constantly taxed on them i.e. no stamp duty, no capital gains tax on selling a second home, etc. We had the impression that we could get ahead financially better than we could back home. We already had a fantastic lifestyle in the UK, lived in one of the most beautiful parts of the country (Herefordshire) and had good secure jobs. Many of the things people do come to New Zealand for (the scenery, space, peace) we already had in the UK. We would have struggled to get a good financial base behind us though. Mostly this was because we felt we were being taxed into the ground, with new taxes springing up everywhere we looked. It was something we were already working towards – finding a way of beating the financial odds, but felt coming here may make the difference. It all looked so simple, going from paying a couple of thousand pounds a year in council tax to less than a thousand dollars a year in rates– it's gonna make a difference, and going from a top tax rate of 40% plus 11% National Insurance to a top rate of 39% - well – we liked the sound of that.

We now live on one salary, and by New Zealand standards quite a healthy one. We are careful with our money but not tight (well – not most of the time anyway) and that should pay off in a few years. We also wanted my parent's lousy UK pensions to go that bit further, and by moving to New Zealand, we figured they would easily be able to live comfortably. They'll still have to be careful just not as tight. So far it's working out reasonably well.

It's often said "No one moves to New Zealand for the money". Well, I have to disagree. It may be true that most people don't, but it's not true that no one does – because quite frankly – it **was** one of our reasons for moving here. So I guess if nothing else – be assured that if your financial stability is important to you – coming to live in New Zealand doesn't necessarily mean you have to give that up. You **can** gain a better quality of life in New Zealand without having to give up your financial security to get it. ☺

IS IT CHEAPER TO LIVE IN NEW ZEALAND?

Factoid:
1 in 5 Kiwis run out of money before payday.

The cost of living here is surprisingly high, given the relatively low wages and the lower quality of some goods. And it is getting higher fast. So I think it's vitally important to bear this mind and take a very honest look at your financial circumstances before you decide where to emigrate.

This is where we fell down in our research. Although we are coping very well now, I did get a shock when we arrived (probably the first 6 – 12 months), even though we'd been to New Zealand twice before. Despite all the preparation work we did - I had a feeling that we would have missed something and it would be big. It was and it turned out to be the cost of living. This coupled with the realisation that we really didn't want to have to curtail our standard of living "too" much. Many people feel that they are quite prepared to "go without" in order to get a chance to live here, but I would caution that being realistic about this is vitally important.

Just what **are** you prepared to do without? Because for a lot of people it's not about giving up flash "consumer items" – it's about affording the bills – especially heating bills (New Zealand houses are notoriously cold!) and the dreaded mortgage. Please don't make the mistake of thinking that money won't be an issue for you because you are happy to buy a 10-year-old car, you won't be buying designer clothes and you won't eat out every night. It's a lot more basic than that for many migrants. Besides – we have a 10-year-old car – and trust me – it isn't cheap to run. And I have only once bought a designer anything – and that was second hand. And yet – we still have to watch the pennies, and there are many things we feel we cannot afford to do here in New Zealand. We are far from the only ones.

There has often in the past been a perception that living in New Zealand is ridiculously cheap because generally speaking – people expect £1 to equal $3. Well, in the five years I've been traveling to or living in new Zealand, the best its been for us is £1 = $2.8 except for a day or two when it actually did hit $3. For most of the time it's been a hell of a lot less than that – often around the $2.50 mark. Compared to living in the UK, it may well **seem** cheap – but bear in mind – you won't be earning £UK, or paying UK taxes – you will be living on New Zealand wages! It makes a huge difference – believe me.

The problem with the "$3=£1" scenario is that many goods are still priced at that, if not $4=£1 or more, while the actual exchange rate just doesn't justify it. However, you won't notice if you get into the rather good habit of not converting everything, because it will drive you mad! I really struggled with this for the first year or so, constantly working out how much items cost in £. I know that those people who accepted straight off that it was pretty irrelevant, had an easier time of settling. I really think that the sooner you can accept working in $NZ – the better you will be.

We are having this problem with flights at the moment. A flight would cost £850 in the UK, but £1000 from here if we pay in $ and convert back to £. From what I can see it's because the £1-$3 rate is being applied for the New Zealand price (looking at Singapore Airlines as an example). That's $625 difference - which is a **lot** of money here. (178 coffees worth in fact 😢.) We recently had to go back to the UK twice for family weddings – believe me – it can hurt!

Hopefully this perception of incredible cheapness will be dulling a little thanks to forums like www.emigratenz.org. We felt that with hindsight (that magical ingredient) the information given at Migration Expo's and online was often "massaged" to present New Zealand as cheap; they just left off the cheerful😊! Looking at the "cost of living" figures we were given by StatsNZ (Statistics New Zealand) before we came here is not even funny. And if you do use those little pamphlets as a basis for whether you think it's cheap here or not – please just bear in mind that very many Kiwi's live in what most of us would consider poverty – and they get included in those statistics. If you use the "Average Household Income" figures, and reckon that earning about that amount you will be able to cope – think very hard. It may not be as easy as you think it is.

According to the Household Economic Survey for June 2007 (which gives the same information that you will find in the pamphlets you can pick up at information days):

- Average Household income was $67,973.00 (that is take home pay of $**948** a week)
- Average household spending was $**980** per week (😢)
- 23% went on Housing and utilities ($224 per week)
- 16% on Food ($156 per week)
- 14% on Transport ($136 per week)
- 10% on Recreation ($97)
- 5% on Household goods and services ($51)
- 3% on Communication ($31)
- 3% on Clothing and footwear ($33)

- 3% on Alcohol, tobacco and drugs (!) ($27)
- 2% on Health ($23)
- 1% on Education ($13)
- 20% went on miscellaneous goods, and other expenditure ($191)

Doesn't make it look too bad, as long as you can get the "average" salary. But bear in mind – statistics are just numbers looking for an argument. Take that housing number for example. $224 a week may not sound too shabby to be spending on a mortgage. But you have to remember that according to StatsNZ – only 35% of households in New Zealand actually have mortgages. Many people either rent – which tends to be a lot cheaper than a mortgage, or have paid off their home loans already– so don't have to pay anything for their house. They get included in that number. You also need to bear in mind that house prices have risen hugely in the past few years, so anyone buying a house prior to about 2004 will have a pretty small mortgage compared to the one you may have to take out to buy a house at today's prices. Incidentally - $224 a week will pay for a mortgage of $115,000.00 at the current rate of 9%. So you need to look at the figures for average spending very carefully. Can **you** live with spending limits like that?

You also need to consider that some things just may not justify the prices, although the same can be said anywhere. It's odd to find that its often cheaper to ship books in from Amazon.co.uk for example, than to go to Whitcoulls, who by virtue of bulk shipping **must** be able to get books shipped here a lot cheaper than me as an individual surely? (As much as I'm very careful with money – my two weaknesses are books and coffee – without which my life would be empty ☺) I also sometimes find the cost of food items in the supermarkets expensive. Partly that can be because the quality of the produce is not always great – and yet it can have a high price tag. This is one of those very individual things though, so you may find that what I think is a lot of money for something, you think is fine.

One thing I think that can really help you get a good grip on your basic living costs is to have a look at some of the supermarket websites in New Zealand. Most of them have "Online shopping" (look for Woolworths and Foodtown) where you can literally pretend to do a "weekly shop" for all the items you would normally buy for your family. Now, look at the total amount of dollars that will cost you. How does that stack up against your UK spend in the supermarket?

> To work that out, simply divide the cost of your "shopping cart" by the current exchange rate. So if your weekly or monthly shop comes to $200, and today's exchange rate is 2.5, then the £UK equivalent will be £80. Would it cost you about £80 to buy the same trolley of food at your normal UK supermarket?

Not only that – but do you know how much of your monthly take home pay you spend on supermarket shopping as a percentage in the UK? If you do, then try looking at that New Zealand shopping bill, and working out how much take home salary you need in New Zealand for it to be the same percentage! Look at how it compares with the Statistics above – are you spending more than the "average" person for you normal weekly shop, and if you are – does that mean you really ought to be also earning more than that?

> First: say your shop in the UK is about £80, and you earn a take home pay of about £1000 a month. To work out the percentage, divide £80 by £1000, and then multiply by 100.
> (80 ÷1000) x 100 = 8%.
>
> So you know that $200 also needs to be about 8% of your take-home pay. To work out the take home pay from that, Multiply $200 by 100, and divide by 8(%).
> (200 x 100) ÷8 = $2500.
>
> So your take home pay needs to be $2500 in order for your food bill to remain the same proportion of your take home pay.

Some things like petrol still seem really cheap to me (at around $1.70 (Jan 2008) a litre – weyhey!) I do feel though that for most people - these costs will be just as prohibitive as they are in the UK, although that doesn't stop people driving gazillion litre 4WDs. However, like everywhere else, the price of fuel is rising fast (it was only $1.20 a litre when we first arrived here as migrants, and was $2.10 by June 2008) and my view on the cost of petrol has therefore become more "colourful" and I'm starting to squeak at the fuel pump. (Note – you can get vouchers for 4-20c off a litre from certain supermarkets. It can be worth buying an extra tin of something to take you up to the next "level" of voucher – but **only** buy things that you would use anyway. Don't spend extra money to "save" money).

When I actually sit down and look back on how much we have spent on things in the last few years, it really is a mixed bunch of whether we feel we are paying more than we would have done in the UK, or less. There are many things we won't pay for here because we don't feel the price is justified by what you are getting. Gym membership is a good example – we happily paid over £70 a month for joint membership to a great gym with a lovely pool. Here most places want about $25 - $30 a week each if not more (around about £36 - £45 a month each), for a basic gym membership with no pool, and old (and often grotty) equipment. In other cases I've found things seem expensive, but then when I work it out, its actually rather cheap, food and entertainment would be a good example. Cheap night at the cinema costs less than $10 each (And if you move to Wellington – head for the Embassy on Tuesday night and get Platinum seats – you won't be disappointed). Decent wines here are pretty reasonably priced. And, because this is really rather a cool place to live – in some cinemas (such as the Embassy), you can combine the two, and get a glass of rather nice New Zealand wine to take into the cinema with you, for less than $40 for two of you. Now that's class!

So, it isn't always wonderfully inexpensive to live in New Zealand, not by a long shot. Even some migrants - for all the money we can bring over from selling our comparatively expensive houses struggle with the cost of living (I mean putting food on the table and a roof over their heads - not going to watch cricket or going to the theatre!) Also bear in mind that if you cannot buy a house outright – your mortgage will be much higher than at home, and house prices are still rising in New Zealand. Mortgage rates have gone up over 2% since we arrived here, and the floating rate is currently at 10.55% ☺ (as at December 2007) and they are said to keep rising for a while longer. Although the housing market here in New Zealand is "cooling", house prices are not actually dropping yet – so if you are going to buy a house – just keep in mind any mortgage costs – you may get a fright! Even if house prices do drop, and interest rates start coming down, even at the best rates, New Zealand rates tend to be few % more than UK rates. Great for savings – terrible for anyone needing a mortgage.

Many people ask on the emigration forums if it's going to be possible to live on $xxx, depending on what job offer they have, or can expect. The problem is you are the only one that can answer that question really. Some people can live quite happily here on an average or even below average wages, and are in Paradise; while some will struggle on over $100,000 a year and find paradise is an awfully long way away. It's swings and roundabouts. It's so much down to what your individual situation is regarding money, and whether or not you are prepared to manage it properly or have no control over it whatsoever.

My feeling is that you should be prepared for a high cost of living and most importantly learn how to deal with your money while you are in your home country, then when you get here you will have the skills to deal with what you find. You will also have a much clearer idea of what kind of salary you **really** need in order to have the life **you** want in New Zealand. It may not always be the same as the life other people "think" you should have when you come to New Zealand.

WHAT ABOUT THE DREADED TAXES?

Intaxication:
Euphoria at getting a refund from the IRS, which lasts until you realize it was your money to start with.
From a Washington Post word contest

Whatever your politics and views – you have to pay them! So before you head over here – let's run through the basic income tax rates.

Firstly – something many of us find odd is that unlike in the UK, there is no "tax free personal allowance" in New Zealand. You pay tax on the very first dollar you earn. Even if all you earn is interest on savings. You also pay tax if you are a child, though despite what many people believe – there is a rebate, which allows children to earn a small amount each week tax-free. I find this really ridiculous, and in a country where so many people are living on incredibly low wages – I find it quite reprehensible. That being said – no political party in New Zealand is promising to bring such an allowance in as far as I know – so I guess we have to live with it.

On the other hand, the good news is that you don't have to pay "National Insurance" contributions in New Zealand – however – there is a small sum on top of your income tax, which is the ACC Levy (Accident Compensation Corporation). This funds compensation and medical expenses for anyone who has an accident in New Zealand (which basically gets you discounts at the Doctors etc, and also pays benefits for those unable to work due to accidental injury). Interestingly – you can get discounts on medical fees through ACC even if you are not a New

Zealand Resident – which can really be helpful – as my family has found to their benefit! ACC levies are also capped so for high earners – there is a maximum they pay. For the year April 07 – March 08 – the maximum payable to ACC is $1297.62 per year which means that any earnings over $99,817 per year do not attract a further ACC levy.

The Inland Revenue (IRD) Website is actually quite helpful and can be found at www.ird.govt.nz. You can easily find the current tax rates by looking on there.

- Go to the Homepage www.ird.govt.nz
- Under the Find Out About box, click on Tax Rates and Codes
- Then click on Income Tax Rates for Individuals
- Now you get this table:

Tax Rates for October 2008 – April 2009		
SALARY EARNED	Income tax Rate	Tax rate with ACC added
Upto $14,000	12.5%	13.9%
$14,001 - $40,000	21%	22.4%
$40,001 - $70,000	33%	34.4%
$70,000 and over	39%	40.4%
Not Declared *	45%	46.4%

*So make sure you get a tax code pronto!

In fact – you can use the IRD website to work out the tax you will be paying on that dream job, and how much money you will have in your pocket once the government has taken its share. Let's pretend you have a job offer for a cool $75,000 a year.

From the home page –

- On the Right hand click ⬚Work It Out⬚
- Click on ⬚Pay as you earn PAYE⬚ in the list
- Up pops another window and you will see a list of Calculators.
- You need the ⬚PAYE / Kiwisaver calculator⬚.
- Next to this it says Start. Click on ⬚Start⬚.
- Click ⬚I am an employee and I would like to calculate PAYE for myself.⬚
- Select the tax year and then click ⬚Continue⬚
- Now you need your tax code – to keep things simple – if you are an employee – it's ⬚M⬚ -you can check codes on the website to be sure as well
- You have to work out your monthly Gross Salary.
- So divide your yearly salary by 12 (Using $75,000 that's $6,250)
- Put that in the first box, and click the button for ⬚Gross Salary⬚
- You can select the pay frequency (which for mine is monthly – if you want fortnightly – then divide the yearly salary by 26 and use that and click fortnightly etc)
- Leave the Kiwisaver Option blank for now

- Click [Calculate]

This gives you the following information:

CALCULATION	
Gross income (Salary / Wage)	$6,250.00
Kiwisaver Deductions	$0.00
Paye Deductions (including ACC Levy) (2008 rates)	$1,675.26
Student Loan Deductions	$0.00
Net Payment (I.e. What ends up in your pocket)	**$4,574.74**

Now you know what you will have to live on and can plan accordingly!

> Note: This is the 6th version of these instructions since I originally wrote this. The IRD constantly changes both the calculators and the steps needed to get to them. Unfortunately they seem to make it more confusing every time. The first time I used the calculators it was very simple. If these instructions do not match up with the website when you go to try this – I do apologise.
>
> There are other ways of finding the information from other calculators on the website – but I find the PAYE calculator is the best one.

There used to be tax rebates available for low-income earners, including children, but these have been removed with the change in tax rates.

It's also worth noting that you should apply for an IRD Number as soon as you come to New Zealand. If you do not do this you will be taxed at the 45% rate.

New tax rates coming in October 2008.

After a long and drawn out refusal to part with any excess money – the government relented and agreed to tax cuts.

The rates are due to change in 3 steps over the next few years (it doesn't do to rush these things), with the changes after October being to the income brackets, rather than new tax rates. Keep your eyes peeled for further changes on this, because if there is a change of government – we may end up with even newer tax rates. The IRD Website will in time have new calculators to take into account the new rates.

It will be confusing for a while – but just work through the calculators slowly and surely and you will get the information you need.

Tax Rates	From October 08	From April 2010	From April 2011
12.5%	Up to $14,000	Up to $17,500	Up to $20,000
21%	$14,001 - $40,000	$17,500 - $40,000	$20,001 - $42,500
33%	$40,001 - $70,000	$40,001 - $75,000	$42,501 - $80,000
39%	$70,000 and over	$75,001 and over	$80,000 and over

So – what about other taxes you have to pay – because we all know it doesn't stop at Income tax!

Well, Instead of VAT – you have GST (Goods and Services Tax), applied to a whole host of things you buy. That's 12.5% (instead of 17.5% in the UK). So that should (in theory) help make things cheaper to buy. Bear in mind though that unlike in the UK, GST is applied to food items! Also, something most of us will I'm sure be quite chuffed about is that Petrol tax is a lot lower in New Zealand than in the UK. In fact if you look at the cost of petrol round the world, most countries actually pay the same price for the petrol itself, it's the tax that each government adds that accounts for the huge difference. Do be aware though – that if you drive a diesel vehicle here – while the price at the pump makes it look real cheap you have to pay a Road User Levy instead which is a cost per mile and is paid twice a year when the WOF (Warrant of Fitness – like an MOT) is done. This is currently $32.79 per 1000km traveled. Information on this can be found at the Land Transport New Zealand Website: www.landtransport.govt.nz

You also do need to pay a car license fee – currently about $180 a year for a standard car. (In fact only about $44 of that is the car tax itself – most of it is another levy for ACC). And while not technically a tax – the WOF has to be done every 6 months on cars older than 3 years – and should cost around $40 a time plus of course any items and labour you need to pay for to get the car passed. So far our WOFs have only cost $40 once, and that was the first one after we bought the car 😊.

And then there are the Rates. Which currently there is a lot of fuss about here in New Zealand because they are rocketing (and not downwards). This is what you pay instead of Council tax. I've heard it said that "There is no council tax in New Zealand" – but really there is - it's just got a different name. It is still the same tax. The rates are based on valuations done every few years on behalf of the local councils. The councils then determine your rates bill based on those valuations. Do look carefully at this when planning your move because as with many things, while the rates look ridiculously cheap compared to UK council tax, bear in mind you need to pay it out of a New Zealand salary! On a side note – we pay much less in rates where we live because we are rural. We have friends living in the nearby town, who own about 1/3 of the house and land we do – but their rates are twice what we pay. The main difference in facilities is that we have to pay a private company to remove our rubbish and we are not on a town water or sewage supply.

On the positive side – you **don't** have to pay:

- Stamp Duty when you buy a house.
- Inheritance tax when you die.
- Capital Gains tax if you sell a second home.
- You will however pay tax on the sale of any houses that you buy and sell with the sole intent of making a profit.
- National Insurance.

You also need to be aware of an odd quirk in the New Zealand tax system that can affect how much salary you should be looking for. Most people don't get such perks as company cars, medical insurance, more than 4 weeks holiday or subsided anything. That's because the company has to pay tax at 33% on anything it gives you, so they tend not to do it. The only exception to this is the new Kiwisaver pension scheme, where contributions from your employer will have a tax benefit for them. So you need to factor these items in when you get that job offer!

So as with just about everything else – you win some you lose some. Overall though – we still feel that the tax burden here in New Zealand is a little less than it was back home. Of course I have no evidence for that. The problem with taxes is so many of them hidden; it would unbelievably boring if I had to actually work it out. And despite appearances, I do have a life. 😊

WILL I HAVE TO TAKE A LOWER WAGE IN NZ?

*"Only in our dreams are we free.
The rest of the time we need wages."*
Terry Pratchett

You will, I'm sure, be told to expect a significant cut in salary from your usual UK pay. Some people take huge cuts in salary, some only small cuts. Very few people manage to get a dollar equivalent of their UK pay. But it **can** be done.

We had to take a large pay cut when we first came here too– a job offer helps sweeten the visa process considerably, so it was worth taking a drop in salary to get into the country. Many companies won't give you a job when you are still in the UK, so for us, a "job in the hand" was worth snatching, even at a lower salary. However it didn't take us long to find out that my husband had been "ripped-off" because we were not Kiwi's. Apparently the person who hired him was dancing around the office because they " …had got this really great guy, dead cheap!" It was pointed out to them that if he were that great it wouldn't take long for him to leave. It seems their theory was that if they hired a migrant they had your loyalty for at least a year. Hubby was determined to make sure that didn't happen without a significant raise in salary.

Well, apparently, the low salary meant they couldn't raise his pay to bring it up to the correct and fair value, because it would have been "too much of an increase". (🤔 We didn't get that either!) So on the basis that he knew the value of his experience; he went shopping for better offers and got three!

These almost reached the old UK rate. This was within nine months of entering the country.

You **can** make a decent salary over here. It's just not true to say that it can't be done. OK, so not everyone can earn big bucks, but then that's the same anywhere. We were earning good wages compared to most people in the UK, and we are earning a high salary here too. In this area, I feel most for the trades people such as electricians and builders, who have to start from scratch and "re-train". If you are in that position – it can be very tough because you cannot get the full rate of pay anyway, as you are effectively unqualified; no matter how much experience you have. For anyone in this situation – the only way is to clamber through all the red tape and get the New Zealand qualification; then you can start earning the real money.

I honestly do not believe that you have to earn less to be happy or that by taking a lower salary you are somehow automatically gaining a "lifestyle". Why can't you have both? What you may have to do is spend less than you earn! As Dickens said:

"Annual income twenty pounds, annual expenditure nineteen nineteen six, result happiness. Annual income twenty pounds, annual expenditure twenty pounds ought and six, result misery".

I have lived and been very happy without money, and I've been miserable while earning a decent salary. However, I also manage to be pretty contented and happy while earning a decent and fair wage. It's just wrong to pay a migrant less than a Kiwi for doing the same job. The same as it's wrong to pay men and women different wages for doing the same job – but I'll stop that one there before I get all huffy.

Almost all companies will pay their employees the least they can get away with. Sometimes it's called exploitation; usually when it happens to other people; so why do we accept it when it happens to us? It doesn't mean we have to take it on the chin if there's a better choice elsewhere. I feel, and it's just a feeling - not based on **any** factual evidence, that there's quite a con going on in convincing migrants that they will have to take massive pay cuts to come here. Whether it's because you "have no New Zealand experience" or "we can't afford high wages here". Fine: we had no New Zealand experience, but hey, we had UK experience by the bucketful and by and large Mr. New Zealand Employer, if you want to be a "world player" you need that experience so pay for it! 😊

Let's be real clear about this: you are getting points on the Skilled Migrant Scheme **because** you have skills and experience that New Zealand **needs** to grow in the world market, but they are going to pay you **less** because of it 😊.

If you have to take a low wage to get here – fine – that's your choice, and I can completely understand the need to do so in a lot of cases. If a low wage gets you the points to fulfill your dream and start your new life, then go for it. Just know that you can move on to something better when you get here. Besides, we have noticed that New Zealanders aren't exactly afraid of moving jobs frequently – it seems to be the done thing in some industries – and certainly in the IT industry which has this interesting sort of revolving door attitude to recruitment and (non) retention of staff.

Please do not be afraid to go in search of better wages. I promise you: it really will not spoil your lifestyle. The only thing that will dent your time on the beach, or tramping through the wilds, is if you are in a job where your employer demands you work long and inflexible hours and pays you diddlysquat. And in all honesty – amongst our friends at least – it's the people on the lower salaries that tend to have the inflexible employers demanding long hours. Once you are here and settled in, look around, see what is available, and what gives you both the money and the time to build the life you really want.

Finally, do be aware that some Migrants have had problems with job offers that include a "Relocation Package". Check the proposed job contract very carefully – some people have found that they are tied into the job for 2 years, and have also found that they are treated rather badly because the companies knew they could not afford to quit the job and repay the expenses. You may find that you sacrifice the chance of moving on to higher wages and a better job because of the relocation package. So think very carefully before accepting such an offer. The same situation can arise if your residency is subject to "Section 18a" restrictions. While this sounds a bit ominous – it is simply a restriction that some migrants get on their Visas (usually if your residency application includes a job offer). All it means is that you have to stay in the same job (or a very similar job) that you were offered for 3 months. It can be a bit annoying if it's a lower wage job – but 3 months is a lot better than being stuck for 2 years. At the end of the 3 months – you apply to have the restriction removed – and you can now be a full time beach bum if you really want to be. 😎

CAN I NEGOTIATE MY SALARY?

If you put a small value on yourself –
Rest assured the world will not raise your price.
Graeme Fowler
NZ Real Estate Investors Secrets

I think it's worth remembering that by and large we are coming out here as Skilled Migrants. Which means we have skills that New Zealand needs. How many of us have skills on the skills shortage list or in an extreme shortage here? So why are we accepting lower wages when our skills, by definition, are in demand?

I picked up a piece of advice about negotiating on house prices, which works when you apply it to your salary too. If you tell the company what you will accept they will not pay a penny more (generally speaking - anyway). But say to them "offer me what you think I'm worth", and then you get to know their price. Bear in mind if they don't get you to do the job, who else are they going to give the job to? There's a shortage of people who can do that job! It takes a strong constitution to do this but it can be worth it, and it did work for us so it may well work for you too.

We were looking at comparison wages and we wanted to earn 3 times our total UK package. It may sound like a lot, but as many goods here can cost more than 3 times UK prices, we figured it was fair. We finally accepted way less than that (nearer 2 times), but then moved up to almost 3 times again, after just 9 months in New Zealand. The next move took place

15 months later, and hubby is now earning more than he did in the UK. Remember – this is three times the **total** UK salary package – you do need to know the value of any "perks" you may get in the UK: company car, private medical insurance, pension contributions, a fifth week of holiday. Don't just look at your UK salary and figure that if you earn £20,000 there, you will be fine on $40,000 or $60,000 here.

The biggest weapon employers have in keeping wages low is our utter reluctance to tell others what we earn. We seem to think it's a dirty word or too personal. It takes some more of that "constitution" but it's certainly worth asking co-workers outright what they are being paid, possibly over a cup of really good coffee! The important point here is to have the guts to say what you earn first, rather than expecting others to answer your question without them knowing what you earn.

So – just to prove what I mean: here are my husband's salaries for working as an IT Security Architect.

1) Hubby earned $90,000 a year to start with plus $15,000 yearly bonus (most of which was actually paid, a minor miracle in itself).

2) He then moved onto $125,000 with a Fuel Card as a perk and a supposed $30,000 yearly bonus (that one didn't appear; turns out the company hadn't paid bonuses for the previous 4 years; always worth asking that question by the way!).

3) He is now earning $152,000 a year but no fuel card. No bonus was promised in the contract, but at the end of the year, he was offered a bonus for an undisclosed amount. Only the bonus didn't appear, and no one was claiming any knowledge of its whereabouts.

Hubby's old boss had just left, and the new boss couldn't locate the mystery bonus either. During what can only be described as "stellar negotiating", hubby sat in front of the new boss keeping his mouth shut and looking "disgruntled". New boss promptly offered $10,000 in bonuses to be paid over the next two months. Not bad really.

We are in the fortunate situation here that hubby's job has quite a small "community" of people who do it and they are often having coffee with each other (coffee really is the source of all goodness in life) so they all know (a) what's going on among the various employers, and (b) what the salaries are. Hubby was recently offered a position through a recruitment firm, so his first step was to buy a coffee for the guy who took the job 12 months ago, when it was last up for grabs (IT jobs really do seem to work on a revolving door basis in this area). He now knew what the guy was being paid and how he earned it. He also got to understand why he was leaving the job and what the problems were. That makes a big difference in deciding whether to go for it or not, and how much you would want to do the same job. This is one area where our typical British reticence really works against us.

But think of it this way – have you ever haggled at a car boot sale? Many people will bargain with a seller over a £1 teddy bear, but won't bargain with an employer over the amount of money their family gets to live on for the next year. And if you know what everyone else is being paid – then how can your boss think of paying you any less?

BUDGETS – THE CUDDLY WAY

Budget: a mathematical confirmation of your suspicions.
A.A. Latimer

The main key to being able to live on **any** wage, whether it's a high one or a low one, is to be able to **manage** your money. Our debt problems came about because we got paid, spent the money and then put blinkers on and earplugs in and ignored the whole thing. Our "Get out of Debt" journey happened because we took the blinkers off, threw the earplugs away, and started actively managing our money. We basically beat it into submission, rather than having it controlling us.

I know many people refuse to "believe" in budgeting, but really, when all is said and done, it's the best way to avoid debt, and live within your means (a very unfashionable phrase these days I guess). Really, budgeting is just a part of Money Management, and to manage your income, you only have to do 3 things:

- Track where your money has been going.
- Work out what you should spend
- Keep tracking where the money goes so you don't overspend.

That's it really.

SO, HOW DO I START BUDGETING? (ARGHHHHH)

> *There are plenty of ways to get ahead.*
> *The first is so basic I'm almost embarrassed to say it:*
> *Spend less than you earn.*
> Paul Clitheroe

Pretty much the first step is to look at what you already do (tracking where your money has been going all this time). You cannot make a change to your finances – if you don't know where your finances are at the moment. There are lots of ways of doing this. The best way is to always "keep accounts" – which is very old-fashioned. It works though. I use Quicken, but there's also MS Money, you could use Excel Spreadsheets, or even seriously old-fashioned paper and pen (if you still remember how to use them). If you don't keep accounts at the moment, then consider it from now on because if you are in a tight money spot, it's worth its weight in crisp dollar bills. But in any case in order to know what you have been spending your money on, you need to list all your outgoings for the last year.

Sit down, grab a cup of coffee and some Tim Tams, (That's Penguins for the "still in Britain" contingent), a calculator and a sharp pencil too, and get to it. You also need a pile of information from the past year's spending – or as far back as you can manage. If that's only a few weeks – don't worry about it – do the best you can. You can get the information you need from bank statements, any receipts you have, your past 12 months bills for things like electricity and phone bills, and pay slips (because you also need to check how much you have coming in). Your bank statements will tell you any charges you have paid to the bank, and how much interest you are being paid or charged. If you already keep accounts, all the info is there already, so this bit is relatively easy.

Now what you need to do is organise that information into a list or table. I find spreadsheets such as Excel are fantastic for this bit. But if you don't want to make one up of your own you can find a really good one at Moneysavingexpert.com:

- www.moneysavingexpert.com
- From the home page – click on Banking / Saving
- Then, under Free Tools click on Budget Planner
- Then click on The Free Budget Planner Itself
- Then pick either the Excel Version which you can save as a file on your computer, or if you don't have Excel, the online version
- Unfortunately – if you use the online version – you cannot save the information.

If you don't want to use the Moneysavingexpert.com version, you can certainly build your own spreadsheet, or just simply list everything. List everything under as many headings as you need - there's a sample list in the next Chapter, which shows you how we categorise our spending: things like Mortgage /Rent, Food, Petrol, Cinema, clothes, whatever headings you need. If you only have 5 headings – it's not enough. The more you break this down, the more accurate your picture will be, and the more progress you can make. This is **really** important. You remember that Household Economic Survey for June 2007? Well, according to that – a whopping 20% of people's spending went on "miscellaneous goods, and other expenditure ($191)". **That** is the bit of spending that usually gets people into trouble. Most people know how much their rent or mortgage is, and what the big bills come to. It's the "other spending" that causes the problems – and it is that bit you need to find out about.

What you need to do is add up everything you have spent on a certain category over a certain period of time– like food for example, and then turn that into a monthly or weekly amount. (Whether you choose monthly or weekly – pick whichever matches how often you get paid. So if you get paid monthly – turn everything into monthly figures).

If you just never keep your receipts – and have no idea how much money you have spent or what you spent it on – then you need to start. So for the next month – record **everything** you spend. Whether it's on a credit card, debit card, cheque or cash – **everything** gets noted. Keep a book and pen with you to make sure you do it. Even a pack of chewing gum gets noted. Then add up all those little or big bits into as many headings as you need – and that's the basis for your spending spreadsheet. An easier way of getting round this is to start your accounts and take the last bank statement or two, and basically use that to get your set of accounts going. Go though the bank statement – writing everything down – who you paid – how much you paid them, the date you paid them, and what you paid them for (If you can remember). Computer accounts programs make this really easy and I do recommend using them! When you have at least a month's information – you can then shove all that into a spending spreadsheet.

The next step would be to "analyse" all the stuff you write down and then look at where and why you spent that money. It's probably time for a top up on the coffee and some more Tim Tams (I think trying to budget is hard enough without worrying about calories as well). Look for things that are costing you money that don't need to. Easy ones to start with off the top of my head are: Bank fees (I have a friend who was paying $15 a month to take $20 out each time from another bank's ATM rather than walk an extra 5 minutes to the banks' own ATM), papers and magazines (I know they are fun but you read 'em in 10 minutes and that's it), library fines (again costing a fortune in some cases as opposed to getting books back on time). Doing this can be a bit depressing - the Tim Tams should help with that - but you may just spot a few things. And also – look at those little bits. Stuff like the odd pack of gum, coffees, lunches out. (I've noticed that many commentators call us the "Latte Generation" and reckon we could all afford palaces if we just stopped drinking coffee. ☺ Go for it if you can – just don't take **my** coffee away from me!)

Look at your regular bills, and see if you can cut them. Are you on the cheapest electricity supply? Can you get your phone bill cheaper? (I'm just changing to Ihug, which will save me nearly $100 a month!) Are you on the best mobile plan (and if you both have mobiles, are they both Vodafone, or both Telecom NZ because it's expensive to call from one phone plan to the other)? If you are in the UK, use www.moneysavingexpert.com to check for cheaper suppliers; in New Zealand – check out www.consumer.org.nz for their Powerswitch pages for electricity comparisons.

The neat thing is in doing this – you can cut your costs without ever having to "Go without" anything. I get exactly the same rights and privileges on my phone calls – it just costs me $100 a month less! And I already know I'm on the cheapest electricity supply because I've checked that too. You may be surprised how easy it is to cut your costs – without having to do without. Budgeting and "living within your means" does **not** have to be painful.

VOIP and Phone calls

One of the items that really catches people out when they first arrive is the cost of calling family back home. Some of us can be terribly homesick, and need to call friends and family for a phone-hug quite a bit. If money is an issue for you, this can make life even harder once you see how much it is costing you. These days, phone calls to the UK are relatively cheap through Telecom; they are capped at $5-$6 for up to 2 hours, or you can call as much as you like for a monthly fee of about $45 (the same system we have with Ihug).

However, if you have access to the Internet, consider downloading a program such as Skype. This is a VOIP system (Voice Over Internet Protocol). You need to have a broadband connection; and a headset or microphone (and possibly a web cam). The person you want to speak to needs the same setup. Then you can "call" each other over the Internet – for free! Skype also allows you to make calls over the Internet to people who do not have access to broadband – via SkypeOut. While this is charged for – it is considerably cheaper than normal phone rates.

Your friends and family can also find non-Internet ways of calling you cheaply from the UK. Moneysavingexpert.com has current best-buy rates for cheap international phone calls from the UK. Some of these even cover calling from UK Mobile phones.

During your first few weeks, if you don't have a phone line, and haven't got Broadband Internet, then I recommend getting a Telstraclear E-Card. This allows you to phone the UK from any phone (including hotel phones) for 4c a minute.

Now you have the bones of a budget. You have tracked your spending, you know how much you spend and on what. You know how much you earn. So, use the headings you have from the first bit of this monstrous exercise and look at how much you are overspending. That is, are you spending more than you earn. (Moneysavingexpert's budget calculator tells you in friendly green or (not so friendly) red numbers where you are over or under spending.)

If you have managed to work out cheaper suppliers for most of your big bills, and you are still overspending then it's time to sit down and decide on what is **important to you** and what you can fairly easily have less of without as much pain and suffering. I could probably manage eating out less, but if someone took my coffee budget away there would be hell to pay. (Imagine The Hulk: "Don't make me angry. You won't like me when I'm angry!") By this point, you should now be getting an actual "budget" or spending plan (in the same way that saying a diet is an "eating plan" is supposed to make it easier to eat a lettuce leaf and a carrot instead of chocolate cake). This is the goal to stick to, what you should aim to be spending on average on all your requirements. Changing habits is not easy but apparently it actually only takes 28 days for something to become a habit. So in my case not drinking coffee for 28 days would get me out of my coffee habit (going a bit far I think).

You also now have enough information to start saving up for your bills in advance. Saving for bills is a great idea, and will make life a whole lot easier once you start doing it. Work out your average monthly bills and put that much aside into a savings account each month, so you always have money to cover them (or do this fortnightly if that's when you get paid as you may do in New Zealand). Make sure there are no fees for your savings account. When a bill comes in, pay it, and move the money from your savings account to your cheque account to cover it. I know for example – that in an average month now

– my bills will be around $900 😱. So I set that aside in a savings account. Some months I don't need all that – so the savings just sit there and in an "expensive" month – there's some extra in there to cover it. This can be really helpful for things like heating bills – where they will be higher in winter. If you know the average over the year – and always put that aside – you should automatically have the money in winter months because you put more aside than you needed in the summer months. This is the very best way to avoid the "How the hell am I going to pay the bills?" panic that sets in now and then.

Next I have to say that I really think the "Sanity Allowance" is a must. This is something that I discovered in Anita Bell's "How to pay off your mortgage in five years", and out of all the things I've learned over the years – this is the bit I credit most for turning me from a spender to a saver. The sanity allowance is basically like pocket money for adults. Both of you get an allowance each payday. Small but something you can spend on whatever you like, without justifying it to the other person. You want to spend it all on chocolate? That's fine 😊. You each have to have the same amount, one of you cannot get more than the other and until you find your feet, this is where all your treats come from. We can budget for meals out and stuff, but if you can't, use the sanity allowance for coffees, cinema, meals out, trips to the spa, or gadgets. It's really up to you to decide what has to come out of that allowance and what you can afford to "budget" for.

And something about budgets: don't think of it terms of "what I can't afford because I don't have the budget for it". Use a budget **to be able** to afford what you want. If you want to be able to go out for a meal once a month then think about what you can do to wangle the money from somewhere. For example: if you are paying bank fees, just think what those fees could pay for if you worked out how to stop paying them! Don't see the need for a budget as a bad thing because it really isn't. It can allow you an amazing amount of freedom from having to worry about how to pay the bills.

It's up to **you** what is important – not anyone else. So don't be bullied into thinking that you "shouldn't" budget for something – just because other people think it's silly. It's your life and your money – and it's up to you to decide how to spend it. Not one of my friends has the same priorities as I do when it comes to spending money. They will buy things I wouldn't dream of spending money on, and I also spend my money on things that they wouldn't buy. And really – do we care? Nope – not a jot. We are all living the lives we want to, and doing it the way we want to. It's not up to anyone else to judge how you spend your money – especially if you can afford to spend it!

I found the first week of our budgeting "boot camp" was the worst- just after we came back from that trip to New Zealand. When you start to look at exactly how much money you spend and what on it's incredibly daunting, and can be a bit embarrassing at first. There may even be an argument or two as you realise what you have been doing in the past. Money worries apparently cause more arguments in relationships than any other subject. So if you are anything like us – you may have a fight or two as you both try ridiculously hard to claim that it wasn't **you** who spent the money, but believe me – getting a handle on it makes life so much sweeter afterwards. Once you start, you may even find it utterly liberating. It's one thing to buy yourself a jumper and then panic because you don't really know where the money is coming from to pay the credit card bill, but imagine what it's like going out to buy a jumper because you **know** you have the money set aside for it.

You may not buy as many jumpers, but the ones you do buy; you are not going to be in a cold sweat over!

I know that makes it sound like I think it's easy, and I do know it's not. But it **is** possible. We have "Budget days" probably every 4 months where we sit down and look at ways to improve what we do (but then I'm a bit daft in the head when it comes to money management☺). The last day we shaved about $150 per month off our spending plan. That is then money we can save for our future.

Finally – it is vitally important that if you are a couple – both of you need to be on board with this and working together. If only one of you is prepared to put the work in and cut down on unnecessary spending while the other doesn't give a toss – you have a rocky road ahead. In our marriage – I'm the one who manages the finances – I keep the accounts, monitor and move the money round, pay the bills, and dole out the sanity allowance and savings – but we both made the commitment to get out of debt and sort the mess out – and are both responsible for making the decisions about what we spend money on and what we don't.

Budgeting and bonuses

I've noticed many people count their yearly bonuses in their incomes when they form budgets, or try to work out why they have no money. There is a problem with this however: what happens if (like Unisys – my husband's second employer here) – the company tells you your bonus is part of your package – and then they don't pay all of it – or indeed any of it? Believe me – we have been on the sharp end of smaller than expected bonuses, and we have seen the sheer panic set in with friends who were relying on a bonus to fix problems with their finances.

So, my advice is: when negotiating salaries – try not to fall for the package including the bonus. The number you need to base your budget on is the base salary only. A bonus – if there is one – is just that – **a bonus**. You may not get it. And the worst thing is that because bonuses are often worked out on company wide results – they often have nothing at all to do with how hard **you** work. You remember that $10,000 bonus that my Hubby's boss said he would get? Well, after it didn't appear the next month, he questioned the boss, and was told that it would now only be $8,000, and he wouldn't get it for 3 months. A serious sense-of-humour-failure followed.

Set your budget based **only** on your normal salary. Any bonus you get can then be used as you see fit. We tend to use them as lump sums to help pay down our mortgage, or to set aside in an emergency fund. We also allow a proportion of it for extra sanity allowance, because hey – if you don't need it to pay bills – you can enjoy yourself a bit with it. 😊

A SAMPLE BUDGET TO HELP YOU SEE WHAT I'M RABBITING ON ABOUT.

"It's clearly a budget.
It's got a lot of numbers in it."
George "Dubya" Bush

This is a list of our spending when we lived in Central Wellington with a single salary of $90,000. Figures are per **fortnight** (we got paid every 2 weeks)

FORTNIGHTLY INCOME		2406 (After Taxes)	
RENT	1080.00	HAIRDRESSER	8.00
ELECTRICITY	35.00	HOUSEHOLD / CLEANING	10.00
TELEPHONE	15.00	HOUSEHOLD GOODS	50.00
BANK FEES	6.00	POSTAGE	20.00
CINEMA	28.00	CARDS & GIFTS	30.00
OTHER EVENTS / GOING OUT	30.00	STATIONARY & PAPERS	15.00
INTERNET	3.00	ALTERNATIVE HEALTHCARE	20.00
SKY TV	3.00	AUCKLAND FLIGHTS	40.00
HEALTH INSURANCE	39.00	GROCERIES	300.00
CONTENTS INSURANCE	16.00	DRINKS	10.00
PETROL	30.00	COFFEE OUT	50.00
CAR HIRE	70.00	**SANITY ALLOWANCE**	**100.00**
PARKING	15.00		
PUBLIC TRANSPORT	24.00	**TOTALS**	**2097.00**
FLOWERS	20.00	**INCOME**	**2406.00**
TOILETRIES	30.00	**DIFFERENCE**	**+309.00**

So – what does this tell you? For a start – hopefully you can see that I have way more categories for spending than the Household Economic survey. And we don't have a "miscellaneous" category. The more you break it down the more accurate the picture you can get and then the easier it is to find where to make cutbacks. This was the budget we worked to when we first arrived in New Zealand, and as you can see – we did actually manage to save some money each payday. At this point – we saved whatever we had left by the next payday. Sometimes we managed it; sometimes we overspent and couldn't make the savings. Often – that was because we ended up spending way more than we should have on coffee – and we ate out quite a bit, which we hadn't budgeted for. Going out for coffee was my way of dealing with the homesickness, and struggles I had with adapting to a new life. Alan worked about 3 minutes walk from our apartment – so it was easy to meet up and grab a drink. And eating out was just so much easier than cooking when it all felt too difficult.

Our phone, Internet and Sky TV were discounted as part of a work package (from Telecom). We were renting a 2 bed apartment right in the center of the Central Business District, which is why the rent is quite high, and why we had costs for hiring a car – so that we could take some day-trips. There wasn't much point in us buying a car at that time.

Since then – having moved and taken on a mortgage, bought a car, and a new job for my husband, we altered our categories, and made them a bit clearer, adding up categories into subheadings. Personally I think there is no "right way" to organise your budgets as long as they make perfect sense to you – because let's face it; you are the one that has to live with it!

MONTHLY INCOME (AFTER TAX)		6500.00	
MORTGAGE	2200.00	HOUSEHOLD	50.00
UTILITIES	**558.00**	HOUSEHOLD / CLEANING	15.00
ELECTRICITY	170.00	HOUSEHOLD GOODS	10.00
TELEPHONE	165.00	FLOWERS	10.00
INTERNET	24.00	SWIMMING POOL	15.00
SKY	36.00	**GIFTS**	**98.00**
MOBILE PHONES	30.00	CARDS	8.00
RUBBISH COLLECTION	28.00	GIFTS & FLOWERS	50.00
FIREWOOD	30.00	CHRISTMAS PRESSIES	40.00
RATES	75.00	**FINANCE FEES**	**117.00**
INSURANCES	**134.00**	WISE PLANNING FEES	117.00
SOUTHERN CROSS HEALTH INSURANCE	26.00	**STATIONARY**	**60.00**
CONTENTS INSURANCE	35.00	POSTAGE	30.00
HOME INSURANCE	47.00	STATIONARY	15.00
CAR INSURANCE	26.00	PAPERS & MAGS	15.00
TRANSPORT	**855.00**	**CLOTHES (NON SANITY)**	**50.00**
PETROL	400.00	NORMAL	0.00
PARKING	50.00	SHOES	50.00
PUBLIC TRANS	350.00	**HOLIDAYS**	**290.00**
SERVICING / WOF	50.00	ACCOMODATION	100.00
CAR ACCESSORIES	5.00	FOOD	80.00
ENTERTAINMENT	**170.00**	SIGHTS & SOUVENEIRS	40.00
CINEMA	90.00	AUCKLAND FLIGHTS	70.00
THEATRE & EVENTS	60.00	**FOOD**	**955.00**
WOMAD	20.00	ALCOHOL	15.00
HEALTH & PERSONAL CARE	**185.00**	BREAKFASTS	30.00
MEDICINES	10.00	COFFEE OUT	100.00
COMPLEMENTARY MEDS	30.00	DINNER OUT	150.00
PERSONAL CARE & TOILETRIES	75.00	EVENING DRINKS	10.00
HAIRDRESSER	35.00	FOOD GROCERIES	600.00
DOCTORS	5.00	LUNCHES OUT	15.00
DENTISTS	30.00	SNACKS	20.00
SANITY ALLOWANCE	**250.00**	TAKEAWAYS	15.00
TOTALS	5972.00	INCOME	6500.00
		DIFFERENCE	+528.00

You will notice that with this budget – it's all worked out monthly rather than fortnightly. This is simply because my husband started getting paid monthly when he started the new job.

Notes on the Budget

We lost the discounts for Internet, phone and Sky, but gained discounted health insurance – which would normally have been $85 a month. We also had a Fuel Card, but we were actually using about $600 worth of petrol a month – it's just that it only cost us about $400 a month. The public transport went up a lot as hubby now commutes to work on the train.

We now had a swimming pool (that's was one of our "dream life" things and just had to be done). The $15 covers chemicals for the pool. I do the maintenance myself as I quite like it actually, but you can budget for a "pool man" if you wanted to. We did spend $1,000 on a pool cover – but we saved up for that – so it doesn't come under a "budget heading".

The clothes and shoes spending – while it was never a lot – we ended up making a "sanity" item, so we don't actually budget for them any more.

Our food budgets are never likely to be small. That's just the way it is – and we have to make allowances elsewhere. We do live in a area of wonderful cafes, and wineries – so what can you do? I really do love the coffee and the Eggs Benny. ☺

As time goes on – we get this budgeting lark better and better. We are not "Natural budgeters" – some people can work out and stick to a budget very easily. For us – it does take some effort, and that is why we need to have "Budget Days" – to help keep us on track. We also review it whenever there is a pay rise (usually at this point because of a new job). At that point we take a day to go through the numbers, check how we are doing and to "divvy up" the oodles of extra money we will have coming in 😊. I try and split any new money between extra mortgage payments and savings, with a small amount being added to the sanity allowance - just because!

AM I A BIG SPENDER?

Don't buy things; buy freedom.
David Futrelle

OK, so you now know what you have been spending – and have done what you can to come up with a budget that tells you what you **should** be spending. Hopefully – it shows that you have money left at the end of each month before you get paid again. So what can you do to make sure you stick to it and don't spend more than you earn? Because let's be honest – a Budget on a sheet of paper is just like a Diet on a sheet of paper. Great – till you see a gooey slice of Chocolate cake and then it's out the window!

Well, one of the best things you can do is to use a **cash only budget** to get you started. This is something that a lot of budget advisors seem to recommend for people who literally spend spend spend. A cash only budget is where you take out a set amount of money each week and that's your lot. It helps by making you **aware** that you are spending money. When you use Credit or Debit Cards, you never see the real money so for many people it helps when they have to count out $20 bills to buy that $400 coat! This can be really helpful in getting over any "consumerist" habits you may have. Moving to New Zealand of itself won't necessarily turn you into a non-consumer. So – if you really are a spender – try it. I've seen this done on TV programs, and sometimes the cash only rule covers **all** spending – including petrol, food and bills. Sometimes it just covers what is known as "discretionary spending" – that's clothes, books, chocolate, coffee etc. Take out in cash exactly what your budget says you need for a week, and live on it.

If Credit Cards are your problem – then as far as I can see – cutting them up is the only way to deal with it. The last thing you need is to add to any money problems by spending on credit cards if you can't afford to pay the full balance every month. At this stage – we aren't looking at paying off credit card debt – just how to stop spending more. You could try the old "stick the card in a glass of water and freeze it so that you have to defrost it before you can buy anything" trick – but I feel that a ceremonial cutting up of the card marks a change from "Over spender" to "Money saver" – and makes a commitment! Freezing the card means that you cannot use the card on the "Spur Of The Moment" and it forces you to think about the spending you are about to indulge in. Personally I think total and utter destruction of the means to spend money you don't have is much more effective – and satisfying. You also need to remember to delete any Credit Card information you may have stored with online shops such as Amazon. There is no point leaving a "back door" open allowing you to keep spending.

Some people use the "Frozen Credit Card" as a means of having some "emergency" funds around in case of – well – emergencies. I know however that for me, I can be pretty creative in making something an "emergency". These days, because we have our money management under control – we have an emergency fund in our savings account – and that means we don't have to go into debt if the unexpected does come up. Aim to set a small portion of your salary aside to start building this up. You need to get a fund of about 3-6 months worth of salary behind you. It will take a fair while for most of us, but you will get there in the end. Believe me – it can take a great weight off your shoulders to know that you have a slush fund to help out when you really need it. And it avoids the need for a frozen credit card, and the space saved in the freezer can be used for something really useful – like ice cream.

We do use a credit card, because it works in our favour to do so due to the type of mortgage we have. The important thing is that I pay off the balance every month in full – and **never** pay interest on it. I'm not spending on the credit card because I cannot afford the items – I'm doing it because I can afford to pay the bill in full at the end of the month. I truly feel that if you cannot pay the balance in full every month – you should not use Credit Cards. They are too easy to get, too easy to spend on, too easy to not pay off, too easy to extend the limit on, interest charges are way too high (especially in New Zealand – interest rates are usually 15-25% (you may get 5-10% for balance transfers)) and way, way too hard to clear if you get into trouble. If you cannot control your spending on a credit card – don't have one. It can be **very** bad for your finances.

When you look at what you are spending the money on, ask yourself:

- "Do I **want** this?" or
- "Do I **need** this?"

If you **want** it, it needs to wait till you have the spare money or it comes out of sanity allowance. If it's a **need**, then budget for it. Then when looking at items you are going to buy, look at the **price,** but also look at the **value.** Ask yourself

- "Is this **worth** what they are asking for it?"
- "Can I buy it cheaper elsewhere?"

- "Would I rather spend that money on something else?"
- "How many hours do I have to work to earn the money to buy this?"

You would not believe how much money I **haven't** spent by asking those questions. Except on coffee which in any universe is worth any amount of money charged as far as I'm concerned. 😋. If you need some help putting this in context, then you may want to look at one of the new tools on Moneysavingexpert.com: **The Demotivator**. It tells you exactly how much you spend on any given item over a year, and how long you have to work to pay for it. It turns out that my Hubby only has to work for 0.6 of a week to pay for my coffee habit – bargain!

As with everything – it is what is important for **you** that matters. Don't be badgered into deciding what your priorities are by other people. For us – it's eating out and coffee. As long as you can afford it – it's no-one else's place to judge what you choose is a need or a want for you. If you feel spending $300+ on a moisturising cream or a few thousand on a swanky sound system for the car, if you have the money, and you feel it is **worth** it, then that's up to you. Just please do not go into debt to get these things. If you cannot afford it – then you cannot afford it. If you cannot grasp that – you really have to cut those credit cards up.

How do I control myself??? Well, when we were in debt I woke up and realised just how much the banks were making out of me. And how ill I was getting because I was so worried about how we were going to pay the bills. Now I don't remember the last time I couldn't sleep because I was worried about how to pay a bill. **That** is what keeps me going, and stops me buying stuff I really don't need, gets the library books back on time and makes me do crazy things like "budget days". After a while I even got to enjoy it! I've recently watched a Money Saving program brought over from the UK, "Your Money or Your Wife". The presenter gave the indebted half of the couple £280 in £5 notes. This was the amount of interest he was paying every month to service the debt on his overspending. She made him throw all those fivers over the balcony of a very tall London building. (Lucky for the two guys we saw walking below!). He was gutted. But it was a good lesson in how much you can throw away on overspending. I always thought a better illustration was to take money that gets "thrown away" on interest or things you don't need – and burn it. Seriously – would you **really** be able to burn £280 in crisp fivers? If you can't – then why would you throw money away on things you don't need and don't really want anyway – let alone on interest for things you can't afford?

In fact – odd as it may sound – one of the most painful lessons we personally received about the amount of money we had thrown away over the years on "stuff" we didn't need, came about purely because we were emigrating. We ended up doing a lot of car boot sales to get rid of stuff we no longer wanted, and to cut down on the amount we would have to ship to New Zealand. Things we had spent pounds on – we ended up selling for peanuts. Coming away from a car boot sale with a couple of hundred pounds is all well and good – but if you spent thousands accumulating all of it – it's just gutting☹! So if you do decide to declutter and go to car boot sales – take a long hard look at what you get rid of, and how much money you just lost. Trust me – you won't want to spend as much money on "stuff" ever again.

HOW DO I KEEP TRACK OF MY MONEY?

Stop wishing for more money and start managing the money you have.
Mary Hunt,
Money Myths That Empty Your Wallet

So, you have done a budget, you know what you have been spending, and you have now decided what you **should** be spending. How on earth do you keep on track and organize everything?

Well, the only way I can do it is to keep accounts. I do this once a week at least. I take all the receipts for everything we have bought, and enter them into Quicken. It doesn't matter a jot what you use: Quicken or Money, Excel spreadsheets or paper and pen. This is what you need to do if you are serious about ensuring that your income lasts till the end of the month and beyond.

I find it staggering how many people will buy things and not take the credit card receipt. Or even worse – take cash out from a cashpoint and leave the receipt for me to have a nosey at!

That aside – whenever you spend money, especially cash – you should take the receipt. Then when you get home – you should enter it into your accounts. This means that at any given time you have a record of exactly how much money you have left in the account available for spending. This is particularly important while in the UK, where spending can sometimes take days to appear in your account. You cannot rely on what the banks say you have available. In New Zealand – there is no 4-5 day wait for things to "clear" so it's a bit easier to tell. But to be honest – I don't trust the banks anyway – so I prefer to have my own record.

We very rarely spend cash now (we don't pay a fee each time we use Eftpos), as we personally found that we would forget what we spent, and the cash just got frittered away. While we tried our best to keep a note of all cash spending – it really just didn't work that well for us.

You also need to make sure you enter all your direct debits or standing orders. This is where the computer software comes in handy – because you can set up monthly payments to enter automatically. I pay as much as I can via direct debits because at heart I'm lazy and don't want to have to bother paying them manually every month. I like an easy life! And that includes not having to type the information into the accounts each month. It's much easier to just click the "Pay" button and have it turn up in the accounts! Time spent not paying bills = more time at the beach. 😎

One of the really cool things about using software to do this – Is that you can "analyse" your spending. This makes your budget days go a whole lot easier and quicker! So when you put a receipt into Quicken you fill in the following information:

- The date
- How you paid for it
    - Cheque number
    - Eftpos
    - Credit card
    - Direct debit etc
- Who you paid – or who paid you (let's look on the bright side!)

- How much you paid them
- What it was for.
    - This can be adapted to your needs – but can be items like Groceries, electricity, phone, coffee, petrol, and more coffee – whatever you need.
    - This is the bit of the program that makes your every-so-often budget days easy – because you can print off reports that divide all your spending into these categories for you.

Now – here's the bit that way too many people **never** do – you have to **balance** the account. ☺

Most people only ever have a cursory scan of their bank statements. And if they do look – they often never look further than the number at the bottom. This is one of the biggest mistakes you can make. If you never check your statements – how do you know if anyone charged you twice for something? Or if the bank has put in a charge you didn't know about? Or someone stole your credit card and bought a TV that didn't get picked up by the bank? Or a postdated cheque that wasn't supposed to be paid till next month got put through early (no one checks the dates on cheques – so postdating is a waste of time these days). The fact is there can be many mistakes made on either your version of your accounts or on the bank's version – (particularly the bank's version.) In the past few years I have had to claim back hundreds of dollars worth of credit card transactions that for some reason or other have been put onto my account twice. So you really do have to take the time to check your version against theirs. There is no point in working for a living – then putting in effort to work out a budget and manage your money – if you then let the banks stuff it all up for you.

BNZ Credit Cards: Why you need to check your statements!

We had a new credit card with Bank Of New Zealand (BNZ), which we only ever made one payment with. We recently had a statement saying we owed $22.50 for some digital photos paid for at an online store.

We queried it with BNZ – who eventually said that we wouldn't have to pay the bill till they investigated it. The "investigation" resulted in them sending us a letter stating that "Should we wish to further dispute the charge, please advise us in detailed writing with your signature (!?) by [Date]. If we do not hear from you by this date, I will presume that you now accept the charge and no further action will be taken."

Well! Along with this utter garbage – we got details of the person who had made the purchase. We were sure it was just a mistake – rather than an attempt at fraud – after all – I assume anyone fraudulently using our card would buy something more interesting than photos. However – we got her name, address, email, and mobile phone number. None of which was in anyway us, nor could it be linked to us.

We sent a snottogram (of epic proportions) to the bank telling them to do their job and figure it out, and in a call to us we found out the following:

- Because it's under $50 they don't bother with any online security checks such as the 3-digit number on the back of the card.
- So anyone who has stolen your card will get away with it if they don't spend up big.
- The bank assumes that the person using your card details is a relative of yours, and so they don't worry about it, even if the name and delivery address is completely different.
- And yes – they do expect **you** to prove that you didn't spend what you didn't spend.

> - Basically what this means is the banks won't bother checking for small purchases that are not made by you.
> - You **have** to check the statements.
>
> By the way – we closed the card down, as BNZ were beyond obnoxious about the whole thing. The lady whose information we were given (in a serious breach of privacy laws), is "having a few words" with the bank and the Privacy Commissioner.

One particularly important bit about this – is that when you move to New Zealand – you will probably have cancelled a few direct debits in the UK before you left. I've heard of several migrants who found out six months later that they were still paying these direct debits. Now – under the Direct Debit guarantees – it's easy enough to get the money back – but it's faff and hassle you really don't need. If you always balance your statements – you would find these things out the first month it happened – and can sort it out faster. (As a side note – when you do cancel your direct debits make sure you tell the bank – then if the companies involved try and take your money – the bank should tell them where to get stuffed!)

Computer accounts packages make balancing (or reconciling as it is sometimes called) easy. In Quicken – when you get your statement – you hit the Reconcile tab at the top of the screen. This now brings up a window asking for some basic information from the statement. If you have done a reconciliation before – it brings up the previous balance, otherwise you need to enter it. It also asks for any charges that have been applied to the statement, and any interest. Once you have done that and clicked OK, you then get a two-part list.

On one side – is everything you have entered into Quicken as your spending. On the other side is everything you entered as your income. In my case – one side is always much longer than the other☺. Now – get a red pen. Look at the statement, and find the item on the Quicken list that matches. And when you find it – click on that item and Quicken puts a tick against it. Then you tick the item on the statement. Keep going through the statement till everything is ticked. In the bottom right hand corner – you have a little box with some numbers in it – this tracks how well your balancing is going. It shows the "Cleared balance" – i.e. what you have ticked off, and the statements end balance – which is what you entered from the bottom of the statement. And then it shows the difference. You need that "Difference" to be $0.00 (or £0.00). That means you have balanced the account and everything on the statement matches everything you entered as spending and earnings.

It doesn't always work out first time. I'm really bad at forgetting to enter items that I've bought over the Internet. And occasionally – even with the best will in the world – I can lose a receipt. However – any item on the statement that I don't have already listed in Quicken – I can at least take the opportunity to find out **if** I really spent it – or if someone else is trying to pull a fast one and buy some more photos.

Once you get to Zero – you can click on "Finished" and you are done! I also then write on the statement that it is **balanced** – and date it.

(As an interesting side note – if you cannot get the difference to say $0.00 and it just happens to say a figure that – if you add the numbers up – gives you the answer 9 – then it means you have written the last two digits in a number the wrong way round. So for example – if the uncleared balance once you have ticked everything reads $1.53, then 1+5+3=9, so check through the list and see if you have written something down wrong – like 1.89 instead of 1.98, or 5.24 instead of 5.42. Strange but true!)

I guess that might sound like a whole lot of faff and hassle when you would much rather be having a coffee or bumming on the beach. But experience tells me that not doing this means you have very little control of your day-to-day finances – and it's often that lack of control that means you end up with no money. Tracking your spending and balancing statements is really the best step to make sure you can afford the coffee and the day at the beach. If you are worried about the time – well – I probably spend about an hour each week doing the accounts now. And I have a **lot** of accounts to deal with. It will take longer at first as you get used to it and learn the ropes – but eventually it's something you can fit in pretty easily.

Interestingly – when I started taking over the accounts at home after that holiday in New Zealand – I found that my hubby – (bless him 😇)- hadn't actually reconciled the accounts for over 12 months. So while he was using Quicken – he wasn't using it properly. It turns out – he didn't really "get" the reconcile bit. It took me two weeks (and a few "colourful" discussions) to sort it out – and I found that according to him – we had about £5,000, which had disappeared into thin air! No wonder we had no flippin money! So it really is important to balance!

It's also worth noting that Quicken at least can deal with more than one currency – which is really smart for us as migrants with money in two countries. So I have my UK accounts and my New Zealand accounts all running on the same file. You can set a default Exchange rate – so it works out most things on that basis – but if you transfer from a UK account to a New Zealand account – it does give you the option of entering your own final $ amount. So, say you are moving £10,000 from your UK account to your New Zealand account. If you have the exchange rate set at $3: £1, then it would automatically assume that you are going to end up with $30,000. However, because it's a bit clever, it realises that you are moving money from a UK£ account to an NZ$ account, and brings up a box that asks you to enter the **actual** $ amount that will appear in the New Zealand account. It's pretty neat really 😊. You can also run different types of accounts – including a cash account. It can be quite a complex piece of software but you will probably only need to use a handful of the functions on it. I haven't got a clue what some of them are for – but it does the bits I need it to – and I can safely ignore the bits I don't need.

So – to recap:

- Keep all receipts when you spend any money – including cash.
- Enter all receipts into your chosen accounts software or book.
- Enter all direct debits and bills that you do not pay directly, in advance.
- Make sure you add the category of spending if using software.
- When your statement arrives – open it! 😊
- Balance or reconcile your account.
- Check any items that do not match up – did you **really** spend it – or have you made a mistake somewhere?
- Anything that shows up that shouldn't be there – get onto someone and get your money back!
- Make a note on the statement that you have balanced it – and date it.
- File the statement in a ring binder.
- Go get that coffee!

DO I HAVE TO GROW MY OWN VEGGIES?

My heart is like an open highway
Like Frankie said
I did it my way
I just want to live while I'm alive.
It's my life
Bon Jovi – It's My Life

When it comes to moneysaving, and living on lower salaries, then there are some people who do very well indeed by going down the route of being more self-sufficient. Whether it's having a veggie plot, so that you don't have to pay sometimes over inflated prices at the supermarket, or raising your own chooks (chickens) and getting your own fresh eggs. (Most eggs on sale in New Zealand are actually barn or battery eggs 😳).

Personally I would rather boil my head in a vat of acid than raise any animals or do any gardening. 😳 But it **is** a valid way of money saving – and for some people it becomes an inherent part of why they live in New Zealand. In fact for some it's one of the very reasons they want to move out here. It's just that for me, I'm not an "animal person", and I hate gardening. So basically – while I could save some more money by doing these things – I would be miserable doing it, and as far as I can see – I've got easier ways of handling the money that I do enjoy. I always look at how much effort I have to put in versus how much money and enjoyment I get out of the process. I would much rather do a quick phone round of insurance companies to see if I can cut my premiums, than go out and weed the veggie patch. I find it easier, and more satisfying.

If however, the thought of phoning round makes you slightly nauseous, and you actually enjoy gardening, and think animals are cute – then consider this as a very possible way of decreasing your spending. Because if you do enjoy it, not only will you save money – but you will get an enormous amount of satisfaction out of it as well.

I think it is very important to understand that in both emigrating and in money management: "One size does **not** fit all". You have to take into account who you are, and look at what will work best for you. Not me, and not anyone else either.

You can also get a lot of information on old-fashioned or "frugal" style money saving ideas off the Internet. This covers a staggering selection– from making your own skin care products, to cleaning without the use of expensive products, to making cheap meals. The list of ways to save money can be quite mind-boggling. I found a great tip here – which is one of the few "frugal" money saving ideas that I do use. With the sheer number of pine trees around – we pick up pinecones from the side of the road and use them as kindling for the woodburner. Not only are they free, but they make really good fire starters, and they smell nice. My hubby also decided on a budget day that there was next to no point at all in paying $15 to get his hair cut, when we could buy a shaver and do it free. We paid $60 for the shaver, and saved nearly $200 in haircuts in a year. I however am sticking to my $80 a time haircuts!

Moneysavingexpert.com has a "Moneysaving Old Style" board on the Forum, which you may find useful. There is also www.simplesavings.co.nz run by a character called Penny Wise. Some of the site is free access; some is to be paid for.

However – this could be particularly useful given that it is a New Zealand site.

Something that you do need to be very careful of in New Zealand, especially if you are trying to be frugal, is that bulk buying is not always cheaper here. More often than not a bulk pack is actually more expensive than buying several small packs. Never assume that buying in bulk will save you money – you really do need to check the prices. This is something that makes me really angry, because it tends to hurt those who can afford it least. Quite frankly – it's a con!

Whether you go for "frugal old style" money saving or not – the choice is up to you. There is no right or wrong way, and you will not be a failure as a migrant if, like me, you do not want a veggie patch. Neither will you be a failure as a money saver if you find you can't stand phoning round for the best quotes. Too many migrants get caught up in believing that there is a right way to live as a migrant – but comparing yourself to others is never a recipe for happiness. No one else lives your life, and what makes them happy will not always make you happy. How **you** save and manage **your** money has to work with **your** life.

WHAT ABOUT BANKS AND BANK CHARGES?

If someone told you they were about to punch you before smacking you; it doesn't make it legal. The same's true with bank charges.
Martin Lewis
www.moneysavingexpert.com
(Regarding unfair bank charges in the UK)

I have to make clear at the outset that I do not accept that bank charges are at all fair. I know all the reasons for them; how can I possibly expect the bank to work for free; they aren't a charity etc, but banks make enough money out of us as it is and they don't need to make any more. You don't pay Whitcoulls $5 (or Waterstones £5) a month for the privilege of being able to go in and buy a book – so why should you pay the banks to hold on to your money. They make money by investing your savings, or charging you higher rates of interest than they pay, when they lend you money.

I utterly object to being charged to spend **my** money. I don't care what they charge or why they do it, it's not **their** money, it's **mine**! It's a principle thing and at the end of the day no amount of justification for charges actually diminishes my feelings on the subject.

Bank fees in New Zealand are ludicrous and applied for the most spurious of reasons. ASB will charge you for having to ask their permission to spend your money! (The Netcode release fee is a charge applied if you wish to spend over $500 via the Internet. (Currently its $500 anyway. It was $2500 when I started banking with them, went down to $800 after an internet "Phishing" attack, then down to a pathetic $300 after another Phishing attack, and has now settled at $500)). This is for "security", theirs not ours by the way. Apparently the banks got stung by fraud and so ASB introduced Netcode. OK we all need security but I have **never** had to ask permission to spend **my** money, not even when I was 5 years old for crying out loud ☺. As it's for their benefit though, (because if you are daft enough to give out your passwords when someone asks for them, the bank loses the money – not you) why do I have to pay? Also, bear in mind that Internet banking seriously cuts the wage bill for banks anyway as they need far fewer staff – so I object to ever having to pay for any form of banking where I do all the flaming work for them.

> **Note**: You should **never** give out your passwords to anyone sending you an email asking for them. For some reason, people do – including giving the information to a "bank" they don't even have accounts with! I really don't understand why this still happens – but it does.
>
> Please don't be one of those people!

The good news is: you can often get around bank charges. Everything in the New Zealand banking system seems to be negotiable, especially once you have a mortgage or an account with $50,000 in (that is – either loans, savings or a mix of both of over $50,000). I have found the very best way to reduce fees is to have what's called a "Personal Relationship Manger" (would have been called a Bank manager when people had easy to remember job titles!) and to have a good one. You can wangle your way round fees, especially service fees such as getting bank cheques and moving large sums of money for bills etc. by asking your "Personal Relationship Manager" to do it for you ☺. And try just saying that you don't want to pay any fees at all. Bear in mind – the more money you have with them (whether it's mortgage debt or savings) the more "flexible" the fees are. If you cannot do this (say for example you haven't brought all your money over and don't have a mortgage yet), careful use of the system can minimise fees even if you can't stop them.

Be aware that getting small amounts of cash from an ATM is **expensive** if you have an account that charges per transaction. You can get charged up to 50c each time. So when you get cash, get amounts that make it worth it. It is always cheaper to get cash back at the supermarket, paying usually only 20c. Never get cash from another bank ATM: on top of the 50c charge, you get another 50c charge and it really adds up. Do that 7 times – that's a cappuccino 😊.

Decide how you handle cash, it's different for everyone, but when we were using a normal bank account here (before we got our mortgage - more on that later) we used cash much more than we did in the UK. There we thought nothing of using our Switch card (Eftpos in New Zealand is the debit equivalent) for sums as small as £5. In New Zealand we had a minimum we allowed of $25, because with some bank accounts – it can cost every time you buy something with your Eftpos card. Sometimes it's as much 20c each time you use your card.

So, if you want to make five purchases on Eftpos for about $20 – it's gonna cost you 20c each time – or $1 in total. Whereas if you took $100 in cash out and used that to pay for your smaller purchases – it would cost you only 50c, or even 20c in bank fees. It may not sound a lot – but it really is these little bits that people don't account for and get shoved into that "Miscellaneous" category accounting for 20% of what people spend. And these small amounts can really add up very quickly if you don't think about it. A coffee will cost you about $3.50. If you have a bank account that charges every time you use your Eftpos card – that coffee will now cost $3.70. Why on earth should the bank get a cut? They don't make the flippin coffee for you! This really comes under the heading of "look after the pennies and the pounds will look after themselves."

In fact – in a bizarre twist that comes under the heading of "…Only in New Zealand…", some coffee shops started doing "Advance Purchase cards" – where you pay say $35, for a 10 coffee card, and every time you order – they mark your card to say you have had one of your coffees. That way, you only pay an extra 20c for 10 coffees instead of an extra $2. This is a very strange place sometimes 😲.

It is worth being aware that fee free banking is finally coming to New Zealand. It's been here a while with the proviso that you keep minimum balances, often $3,000-5,000. Now some of the banks are offering no transaction fees on their current accounts without the minimum balance requirements. These still tend to have a monthly "Base Fee" though. In some cases you can get no monthly base fee by opting out of being sent paper statements. I'm personally not so keen on that idea, but that's because for me the statement arriving tells me its time to balance my accounts. It's also worth noting that if you ever need a business account – you **must** still get the printed statement for your tax returns – taking a printout off the internet is not suitable for that. You have always been able to negotiate your fees here, but it has tended to rely on having a lot of business with the bank (savings or mortgage or business accounts), but this change means the fee free (or at least cheaper) banking is open to more people, not just those of us with a fair amount of money tied up with the bank 😊. I always thought it a bit off that the richer you were, the less you had to pay in fees, whereas the people who by definition cannot really afford to pay, have no way of avoiding the charges. And it's ironic that all this is happening around the time that Fee Free Banking is coming to an end in the UK.

Current ASB charges (December 2007):

Streamline account (a basic current account):

- $3 a month base fee (waived if you have "Statement Stopper" which means no statements get sent to you by post)
- $1 a month for a Netcode token
- 25c each day you use Netcode
- $2 to set up an automatic payment or bill payee.
- $3 every time you want to pay in cash over the counter
    - This can cause a headache if people pay you cash for Trade Me sales for example – so be careful!
- Fastcheque is now free.
    - (This is an "Electronic cheque" and the best way to pay one-off bills by the internet – use this to pay for Trade Me items – the New Zealand equivalent of Ebay)
- Credit Card Fee from $12 – $40 each every 6 months.
- Credit Card Reward Program costs $10 each for 6 months
    - Don't get me started on why you have to pay for the reward scheme – but check you can get enough points to make it worth it. Currently – you get 1 reward dollar for every $150 you spend. So to earn $10 – you need to spend $1500. That's before you start accumulating enough points for a stick blender!

It's worth noting that in over 3 years in New Zealand – I have yet to write out a real cheque. Every time you write one – you pay a tax on it. Seems a bit silly to me. But basically I just don't write them anymore – I do everything with bill payments or Fastcheque (which do not have the tax on them).

TREE HUGGING AND THE CONCEPT OF MONEY

This planet has - or rather had - a problem, which was this: Most of the people living on it were unhappy for pretty much of the time.
Many solutions were suggested for this problem, but most of these were largely concerned with the movements of small green pieces of paper, which is odd because on the whole it wasn't the small green pieces of paper that were unhappy.
~Douglas Adams
The Hitchhikers Guide to the Galaxy

1. LOOK AFTER THE PENNIES

If you show money the respect it deserves today, and carry it through in all your actions, then one day, when you can no longer take care of it, your money will take care of you.
Suze Orman,
Women & Money

There is a theory that when you start to respect money and look after it, it kind of decides it likes your company and you get more of it. I know it sounds a bit wishy-washy but it really seems to work. Once I got the ball rolling and stopped overspending, the amount of money we had just kept going up. Now that may sound obvious to some when you put it like that, but I can tell you it actually came as a bit of a shock to me. And anyway - if it's really that simple, why are so many people broke before payday?

Not only that – but we really did start getting some unexpected "bonuses". Whether it was overtime payments – bonuses from work we weren't expecting – even an insurance payout (not that I advise getting your car pranged in order to make some money – it was a bit extreme – and I would much rather have had the car and no bruises!)

It's actually (completely non-tree-hugging) compound interest that makes the first bit of that work (and conversely makes debt spiral out of control so easily). Say you have $100. That earns $1 interest the first month. But if you don't spend any of it, the next month you earn $1.01! You just got a pay rise! Your money is multiplying because you looked after it. I can only put the second bit with the bonuses down to Karma or something – because there is no mathematical formula to account for it as far as I can tell.

2. FINANCIAL SECURITY

> *"The more you seek security, the less of it you have. But the more you seek opportunity, the more likely it is that you will achieve the security that you desire."*
> Brian Tracy

I was reading a book a while back, Rich Dad Poor Dad, by Robert Kiyosaki, that had something to say about Financial Security which kind of had the effect of walloping me round the head and made me look at it a very different way.

Many people are in search of either "financial freedom" or "financial security". Kiyosaki maintains that basically you can have security **or** you can have freedom. Seldom do they go together. You can have a good job and the security that comes with a steady paycheck, but it won't often give you financial **freedom**. For that you often need to step outside the box and do something very different with your personal finances. It can mean changing a lot of preconceived ideas about money and that is **very** scary.

Mind you, so is emigrating. As soon as you actually decide to emigrate, you are stepping out of the box. You are daring to actually do something which most people only dream of. Most people live life in an "it's alright for you" kind of daze, if only they had your money / family / background / eye colour / shoe size; then they could do the same. You are not doing that; you are going for it, and you are living the life that you dream about. If you can do that and move half way round the world, why not make a change in your financial "box" as well?

3. THE WAY YOU THINK

> *If you think you are too small to be effective-*
> *You have never been in the dark with a mosquito.*
> Anon.

Many of us really need to change the way we think about money. It's not an evil thing and having it won't turn you from a nice loving, giving person, into a greedy megalomaniac who would sell their own family for a fast buck. Conversely, being poor as church mice won't necessarily make you a decent human being either. Either you are a good person on your own merits or you are not. Your bank balance doesn't alter that. Not a jot!

However the tree hugging principle says that if you think only evil greedy people have money, you won't be able to keep it, because it's going to make you feel bad. If this applies to you, then please just think about it. Most of the people I've met on this journey, some of whom are seriously good at financial "stuff", all started in the same boat as we did, flat broke and depressed about it. The only thing that made a difference is that they felt they were worth the effort and did something about it. Their wealth has not made them different people – it's just made them wealthier people. They have been incredibly generous with their time and in sharing their knowledge. One thing they are not is bad people.

Nowhere is there a law written that says if you become wealthy you also have to become a complete plonker.

4. COME TO NEW ZEALAND TO BE POOR

> *Wishing for crayfish won't bring it.*
> *If you want crayfish – go crayfishing.*
> Graeme Fowler
> NZ Real Estate Investors Secrets

It occurred to me that too many people buy into the "no one comes to New Zealand to get rich" thought process. Well, I've already said that in fact we did come here to get rich(er). In fact – it never occurred to us to even **think** we would be worse off in New Zealand. And guess what – we ain't! You see there's also a school of thought that says what you think about – is what you get. So if you consistently repeat that you will be hard up when you get here – you probably won't do much to change that state of affairs – because well – no one gets rich by coming to New Zealand – so why bother?

We had never heard that idea until after we had been here a while, so just carried on doing what we were doing, and looking to improve our financial skills and standards. And it worked. With knobs on. I can honestly say – the only people who have **ever** said to us that "no one comes to New Zealand for the money" are in fact other migrants. No Kiwi has **ever** told us we cannot make money in New Zealand and most of the Kiwis we know – are also doing their very best to become wealthy – and they are succeeding.

I also have to say that I have indeed met some seriously wealthy people here in New Zealand. Some of them are migrants like us; some are born and bred Kiwis. Some have degree level education; some have almost no education. And I can tell you that not **all** Kiwis drive round in beat up old cars, live on the breadline, never go on holiday unless it's free, and only buy cheap food and clothes. Many do, but it's not all like that.

So, if you want to come to New Zealand, and don't want to be poor – then get yourself educated – take control of your finances, don't accept low wages, and keep moving onwards and upwards.

By the way – just to clarify – I don't buy into the "think about it and it will appear" school of thought. I do however believe whole-heartedly in the "think about it – do something about it – and it will appear" school of thought! The doing bit is pretty important.

DEBTS – HOW TO DEAL WITH THEM AND GET THEM FROM AROUND YOUR NECK.

The Sale of Debt
Debt has been sold to us so aggressively, so loudly, and so often that to imagine living without debt requires myth-busting. Debt is so ingrained into our culture that most Americans can't even envision a car without a payment ... a house without a mortgage ... a student without a loan ... and credit without a card. We've been sold debt with such repetition and with such fervor that most folks can't conceive of what it would be like to have NO payments.

Dave Ramsey,
Total Money Makeover

How Common Is Bankruptcy?
Bankruptcy has become deeply entrenched in American life. This year [2003], more people will end up bankrupt than will suffer a heart attack. More adults will file for bankruptcy than will be diagnosed with cancer. More people will file for bankruptcy than will graduate from college. And, in an era when traditionalists decry the demise of the institution of marriage, Americans will file more petitions for bankruptcy than for divorce.

Elizabeth Warren and Amelia Warren Tyagi,
The Two-Income Trap

I don't want to walk across hot coals because it is fun, but if I can be shown how a short, painful walk will do away with the lifetime of worry, frustration, stress, and fear that being constantly broke brings me, then bring on the hot coals.

Dave Ramsey,
Total Money Makeover

So what are you going to do about it? Whine, complain, continue feeling sorry for yourself? I have a better idea. Get mad! Decide once and for all that you will not sell your soul to the likes of MasterCard and Visa — not one more day, not one more purchase. Get righteously indignant at the very idea of transferring your future wealth to creditors. Repeat after me: I've had it, and I'm not going to live on credit anymore!

Mary Hunt,
Live Your Life for Half the Price

DEBTS – DO I PAY THEM OR LEAVE THEM BEHIND?

*Those who understand compound interest – collect it.
Those who don't understand it – pay it.*
Anon

Debt problems can be crushing. ☹ Compared to many – our debt was actually quite small, and yet I well remember the panic and sleepless nights that having the debt caused. So many people are literally crippled with fear at the size of their debts. They can't sleep, they can't function and they spiral down in to a very black pit. Hopefully, the size of the problem now is not too big a task for you to deal with. So: if you have debts, do you get rid of them? Or emigrate anyway and hope for the best?

Will your debts back home follow you to New Zealand? Too right they will, with enough certainty that I wouldn't risk it if it were me. We actually found it quite difficult to get answers on the status of debts left in the UK and whether you would be hounded if you moved to New Zealand and tried to walk away. We had friends in a situation like this, and we found that we couldn't get a straight answer from the usual places that help with debt problems.

From what we could find out any debt stays "live" in the UK and will go to debt recovery agencies, from there it goes to lawyers! A problem can occur if you leave a UK forwarding address (for example your parents). If that happens the debt recovery services can start ringing them to find a forwarding address for you. Worse – they could start visiting your parents to repossess anything that may be yours. If there is a forwarding address direct to New Zealand then the debts could potentially follow.

We certainly found that when applying for mortgages or credit here in New Zealand – the credit check agency (Veda Advantage) do not look outside New Zealand to see if there is a debt problem back in the UK. So having debt at home doesn't seem to hurt from that point of view. However – the world is getting to be a **very** small place – and it's quite probable that as time goes on – debt recovery agencies will not stop at the edge of the UK when chasing your debts. We have heard from other migrants that credit card companies, finance companies and debt agencies can and will track you down in your new home and start asking for the money you owe.

If you owe money to the government; taxes, fines – well – they are not too likely to leave you alone either. Always remember – the Inland Revenue wants it's money. And they have unlimited funds to use in getting it back (that would be the taxes of the people who don't owe them money 😵!). So it seems that at the end of the day it really is not as easy as just walking away. You may get away with it, equally you may not and the results of that are much more expensive, both in money terms and in stress and hassle.

As far as I can see – and talking from my own battle to kill the debt – you are much better off clearing the debt in the UK while you are still over there. If you try to do it after you have moved to New Zealand – you are at risk of problems with the exchange rates. If you know that getting rid of your debt is going to take £100 a month; some months that will cost you $250, sometimes as much as $300. Now that is fine if you can afford to always pay the $300 – but what if you can't and some months you cannot keep up with your debt busting plan? I really believe it is worth taking a bit longer to get over here, and use the time to get your debts dealt with. Start your new life with a clean slate!

So, if you have debts that you feel you cannot pay off without some help, my advice is to speak to the following agencies while still in the UK. All are confidential and will not cause further problems for you by speaking to them. If you fall into this category – please believe me – you will feel a whole lot better after you get some help on this.

(1) MONEYSAVINGEXPERT.COM

- www.moneysavingexpert.com
- From the homepage – click on the tab for Cards & Loans
- From there, click on
- Debt Problems: Where to start, what to do, where to get help

Look here for general information on dealing with problem debt. This includes how to ask about things anonymously, which is what you really need to do to start. It covers all levels of debt problems – whether you can afford to pay them off or not.

Also on Moneysavingexpert.com, is a forum for Debt Free Wannabies you may find useful. It has a huge amount of really good advice from people already doing it! Go on there to get support, help, and when needed – a kick up the backside!

In fact – if you are at all interested in sorting out your finances – and are looking for savings tips, debt tips or just plain old useful information – this is one website which is full of it.

If you are in what Moneysavingexpert terms as "debt crisis" where you cannot afford to pay your minimum repayments, then you need to speak to:

(2) CITIZENS ADVICE BUREAU.

Each branch has access to a debt advisor and a lawyer often employed via the local authority. They are experts in the debt side of things and they know where else to send you to for help and advice.

(3) THE CONSUMER CREDIT COUNSELING SERVICE

www.cccs.co.uk
(0800 138 1111)

Particularly recommended by the Moneysavingexpert.com website. They can help you in dealing with the companies you owe money to. You can work with CCCS either online via their website, or their free phone helpline – talking directly with one of their counselors.

(4) NATIONAL DEBTLINE

www.nationaldebtline.co.uk
0808 808 4000

All three of these provide **free** personal advice, and can help you sort out your debts, start dealing with them, help with budgeting advice, and come up with a debt management plan. I think it is well worth speaking to all of them and find out which you feel most comfortable using. All of them are confidential, and will not judge you or make you feel stupid. If you are anything like me – you may feel completely embarrassed to have got into such a mess – but getting over that embarrassment is a must if you want to get out of it. Believe me when I tell you: you will not feel stupid when the last debt is gone!

Bear in mind that if you don't learn to deal with debt now, at some point you are going to have a much bigger problem to deal with 😳. Debt never gets smaller unless you work at it. In fact – it gets bigger – and that can happen real fast! Compound interest works against you when you are in debt – in a big way.

These agencies deal with UK debt only – so they are no good if you find you accumulate debts in New Zealand. They also cannot help you if you have debt in the UK but live in New Zealand. So get in touch with as soon as you can (now is good) and get started. The problem won't get better until you do.

GETTING RID OF DEBT IN A NUTSHELL

*"Some debts are fun when you are acquiring them,
but none are fun when you set about retiring them"*
Ogden Nash

If you go down this route then the way to do it is to get your interest payments as low as possible: negotiate with the companies you owe money to (your creditors) if you can and swap money onto cheaper credit cards if possible. Moneysavingexpert.com will have good info about which Credit Cards are cheapest. Swapping debt onto cheaper credit cards is known as becoming a Credit Card Tart 😜. Just be aware that being a Credit Card Tart doesn't really work that well in New Zealand – because our idea of a "cheap" credit card rate is still about 5%-8% for balance transfers - and you still have to pay fees 😒. (Check out www.interest.co.nz for all interest rates on credit cards, mortgages, and savings accounts). Compare this with the UK where it has been possible to get 0% interest credit cards, and you can see that it is quite a bit easier to do this while you are still in the UK.

Do not consolidate with a Debt Consolidation Agency; it makes matters worse in almost all cases. You know – the ones that advertise on telly – saying that it will reduce your monthly payments to a manageable sum **and** leave you enough to go on holiday or buy a new car! Treat these ads with utter contempt. I mean: you have a couple on there; in debt to their eyeballs, can't sleep and they yell at their kids. Yet they just took out an even **bigger** debt and went on holiday???? Yes: their monthly payment went down; but they now owe **more** money than they did before; and the only reason the payment is low is because they are now going to be paying it back over a **very** long time. Which means that in the long run, they are going to end up paying much more money for the debt than they thought imaginable. **Never** pay off debts by taking out even bigger debts.

Actually – if you want to check this out – use the Mortgage Calculator on the Westpac website (www.westpac.co.nz). I know it's for mortgages – but who's counting? The calculator just tells you the payments for a given debt whether it's a mortgage or a car loan or a credit card.

- From the home page: www.westpac.co.nz
- Under Buying a house, click on Calculators
- Then click on Fine Tune Your Loan (this is the best calculator I have found for comparing two different loans).

Just try putting in the details for a £10,000 loan in both sides of the "Fine Tune" calculator. Give one of them a 15% interest rate over 5 years, and one with a 5% interest rate over 25 years. What happens???? Also, let's assume that the very nice people at the consolidators are going to give you an extra £1,000 to spoil yourself – what difference does that make?

Loan amount	10,000	10,000	11,000
Interest rate	15%	5%	5%
Term of loan	5 years	25 years	25 years
Monthly payment	237.90	58.46	64.30
Total interest paid	4,274.00	7,538.00	8,290.00
Total amount paid	14,274.00	17,538.00	19,290.00

So basically – while the monthly payment looks great (you will be "saving" £179 every month!), you now have an extra 20 years of being in debt to look forward to, and it's going to cost you £3,264 extra in the long run. And what about that extra £1,000? Well, it's going to cost you and extra £752 in interest! It had better be a good holiday! And what happens to that £179 a month you are not paying in debt repayments? Is it getting saved? Invested? Is it just not getting spent? Or is it being spent anyway, just on more bills or buying stuff you can't afford in the first place?

If you go to Moneysavingexpert.com and select one of the agencies they advise, or even do it yourself following the advice and guidelines on the website – you may find you can negotiate the interest rates and monthly payments down to workable levels without ever extending the debt, or paying higher and more interest over the long term. Paying **more** interest is not the result you are looking for.

If the debt looks like it is going as far as a debt collector, approach the company and ask for a settlement figure, if they come back with a reasonable figure and you have any spare cash (some people do) or can borrow interest free from a relative, pay them off. (Personally I am not a fan of borrowing from family – as in many cases it can cause huge rifts further down line – but this is very personal – some can do it – some can't). You do **not** have to do this alone. The free debt agencies can and will help you with this – in fact they will negotiate for you and do what they can to organise lower repayments, settlement figures, lower rates and payment plans.

Do not attempt to get some savings behind you while you have problem debt on your hands.

If you can afford to put money aside in a savings account or investment – then you should be using that to pay off your debt. It is extremely unlikely, unless you have the investing skills of a genius, that you will earn as much on your savings as you will be paying on your debt. The only debt you should allow yourself to have while still saving – is a mortgage.

Finally if you do try to pay it off, still allow yourself and your partner a "Sanity Allowance" each month (see budgeting). It may have to be small but it really helps keep the sanity alive. You are much less likely to go off the rails if you have just a little money you can spend on yourself and not the debt.

In-a-nutshell Debt Snowballing:

1. **Draw up a list or table of debts**
   You need to have the following information:
   a. The name of the company
   b. The outstanding balance
   c. The interest rate
   d. The minimum payment

2. **Put them in order. The debt with the highest interest rate goes first.**

3. **Swap as much debt as you can onto lower interest rate credit cards or loans.**
   0% interest is good!
   Use Moneysavingexpert.com to find out the best interest rates.
   Keep a beady eye out for fees and charges – they will not help you get debt free!

4. **Consider selling some of your worldly goods.**
   Bear in mind that you are planning a new life anyway – and many of us seem to go through this whole "declutter exercise". You may as well start now and use the proceeds to pay off some debts and get the ball rolling. Use it to pay

down some of the worst debt – or to pay back any small sums you owe to family or friends.

5. **Try to negotiate lower rates and fees on all your debts that you haven't swapped**
Ask debt agencies to help with this if you need it. My understanding is that companies you owe money to and are having problems paying back, would much rather you phoned them and talked to them than ignore them, so they won't shout at you. That does not however make it easy to pick up the phone. If you cannot face it – call an agency.

Now is where you start paying down the debts – by Snowballing them ☺.

6. **You need to pay the minimum payments on all debts.**
This is where strict budgeting may be needed – to ensure that you can do this. If the minimum payments are just not manageable on your incomes – then you really do need to get some help and it's back to the free agencies.

7. **You can either try and increase your income – or get help to tighten your budget.**
Moneysavingexpert.com is again a fantastic resource for this – the people on there can budget like Anita Bell – though be warned – they don't always take prisoners if they think you are not being as strict as you could be.

8. **Then find that bit extra and pay that onto the first debt.**
(The one with the highest interest rate).
This is where it gets a bit cool (well –I think so!) You see, the minimum payments aren't really designed to help you pay down the debt: they are designed to make sure the bank squeezes interest from you for as long as humanly possible,

so you really need to pay a bit extra to actually get them gone.

Again, it really does come down to having to budget for this bit of extra cash. There is no easy way out on this one. Sit down with a cup of coffee and make some decisions. Try to get at least twice the minimum payment.

9. **Once the first debt is dead and buried, take the WHOLE of that payment, and ADD it to the minimum on the second debt on your list.**
All the time you were working on clearing the first debt, you were paying small amounts off the second one. Now you are going to add another chunk of money to that second debt and pay it down faster.

10. **Once that is gone take the whole of those payments (2nd minimum + 1st minimum + extra) and add it onto the third debt, and so on.**
You have kept paying the minimum on the third debt the whole time you have been paying down those other debts – and this one is going to be buried with those real fast now 😊.

It's called **snowballing** because the further down the debts you go – the faster you pay them off. Moneysavingexpert.com has Internet links to some "snowball calculators" which can help you determine the order in which you should pay off debts if you have more than one. Although its generally worked out that the debts with the highest interest rate gets dealt with first – I've certainly heard of people who actually clear any small debts first – just to get started – so consider that if it fits better. This works especially well if you can negotiate a much smaller "Settlement figure" and pay off any debts immediately, or if you owe friends and family. Nothing can sour a friendship like owed money! Then use snowballing to handle the rest.

However you do it just remember: you will start off **slow**; but when you get going; the effect speeds up and you can watch with some real satisfaction as those debts bite the dust faster and faster.

I have to say, harsh at it seems, pay off the debt. You spent it. It's not right to expect others to pay it for you and that's what happens when you go bankrupt or run away from the debt. Someone has to pay that money and if you don't, then one way or another it gets passed on to other people in the way of higher charges/costs and that's not right. Pay it off and I pretty much guarantee you will think real hard before incurring that much debt in the future. You will also learn how to cope with money and that will make your life here so much easier. I learned the hard way not to spend money I didn't have, and it's been utterly priceless knowledge here in New Zealand.

The Two-Income Trap

Since originally writing about this topic – I have read an interesting book about bankruptcies in the USA. It's called "The Two Income Trap", and according to the authors Elizabeth Warren and Amelia Warren Tyagi, most of the bankruptcies that are occurring now are not because of overspending on consumer items and living it up as most of us assume. In fact – they are due to people taking on larger mortgages and using credit cards to pay daily bills and living expenses. They are occurring because modern life has dictated that most of us need two incomes to pay for increased housing costs, increased food costs, schooling costs, and healthcare etc. Problems occur when one of those incomes is no longer there: either through divorce; redundancy or ill health. So just maybe: having a harsh view of people who get into debt that they cannot pay off – is unfair. Our debt was completely from overspending but many people are not suffering from that cause.

Anita Bell recommends using any second income you have solely for the purposes of paying down debt, paying extra off a mortgage, or if you have neither of those for saving or investing. Most importantly – she recommends you do not use a second income to live on for every day bills and expenses. That way you avoid issues if one of you cannot work – exactly the trap Warren and Tyagi are talking about.

Interestingly I've never actually been in the two-income trap. Whenever we have applied for a mortgage we have only ever used my husband's income to work it out on. It's meant that we couldn't have the best house but it did mean we could cope with the mortgage. It also means that should we ever have children – we don't need to panic about losing an income. Any money I do earn now – we do in fact save or use to pay extra off the mortgage. We do not **need** it to pay for our daily living expenses. That one decision has given us a huge number of choices that many people do not have.

MORTGAGES IN NEW ZEALAND

"Normal is getting dressed in clothes that you buy for work, driving through traffic in a car that you are still paying for, in order to get to a job that you need so you can pay for the clothes, car and the house that you leave empty all day in order to afford to live in it."
Ellen Goodman

Your home: if you choose to buy rather than rent, it's going to by far the most expensive purchase you make here (unless you have a **very** expensive taste in cars). It's well worth understanding how mortgages work, and how the house buying process works in New Zealand. Both have differences to the usual ways of doing things in the UK, and some of the differences are a bit mind-boggling.

Our personal financial journey was completely tied in with finally understanding that as well as not needing to live off credit cards – that we could relatively easily pay off a mortgage early. At no stage in the UK when we had a mortgage had anyone ever told us we could do that – and of course we never figured it out!

Although I'm not really discussing visa issues and the actual emigrating process in this book – it's probably important to clear up what mortgages you can get with what visas. So: if you have a residency visa; not a problem – banks will love you and want to lend you oodles of cash. If you have a work visa: then banks will still lend you money for a mortgage – but they

may require higher deposits. Even then – it is eminently possible to get 100% mortgages with only a work visa although you would probably have to discuss this with a mortgage broker rather than organizing it directly with a bank.

As with almost all of your emigrating experience, much of this depends entirely on your personal circumstances. There are no hard and fast rules.

CAN I GET A DECENT AFFORDABLE MORTGAGE?

*People are living longer than ever before,
a phenomenon undoubtedly made necessary
by the 30-year mortgage.*
Doug Larson

Well, I'm a sick puppy 😋; I think mortgages are really interesting once you understand how they work! The Anita Bell book "How To Pay Your Mortgage Off in Five Years – By Someone Who Did It In Three" is really the best thing there is for explaining it all and reading that will put you streets ahead when you have to go asking banks for shed loads of money to buy your own piece of beachfront New Zealand.

The main options for mortgages are:

- **Fixed Rate Mortgages**

(Fixed for 6 months up to 5 years – some now for up to 10 years)
With this you pay your mortgage as normal – a fixed amount each month, some of which is paying off the balance of the loan, most of which is interest.

- **Flexible Rate Mortgages**

(Your bog-standard old-fashioned normal type mortgage).

Again – you pay a fixed amount each month – the payment being mostly interest and some of which actually reduces the debt. The interest rate changes in line with the rates set by the Reserve Bank of New Zealand (equivalent to the Bank of England).

- **Revolving credit accounts.**

(See below – they need a chapter all to themselves, because they are a bit odd if you are not used to them.)

- **New – Offset Mortgages**

Offset your savings against your mortgage and therefore pay less interest. This is a bit like the mortgages you can get from the Woolwich or First Direct.

Be aware that you can split your mortgage into chunks here, fixing some for different lengths of time, having some on a normal flexible mortgage, or some on a "Revolving Credit" (See next chapter). This is something I found really bizarre, because we just don't have this in the UK. But to be honest I really like it. I just split mine into 2, but you could do a three way split: say some on Revolving Credit, a one year fixed rate, and a two year fixed rate, or even more – whatever suits you. It means you have a bit more flexibility to work with interest rate changes, and by splitting the mortgage up you can pay off your mortgage faster by making the overall interest rate lower. For us, we started out with a total of **$265,000.** We split that by having $100,000 in a Revolving Credit mortgage, and the rest we had in a Fixed Rate mortgage.

Firstly remember: it's **always** worth negotiating with the banks over your mortgage. The more you need to borrow the more clout you have, so don't be shy. The worst that can happen is they say no and they may well say yes! If you don't ask: you don't get.

Tell them what you want – and see what you get. With our original mortgage here I got 0.5% off my variable rate on the Revolving Credit mortgage (that's the ASB Orbit account) and I also negotiated a refund on the monthly fee of $10 (now $12) but forgot to negotiate a refund on **all** fees, so I do still have to pay $2 a time to set up automatic or bill payments. 😊 I'm currently paying 10.25% instead of 10.75%, that's on the Revolving Credit mortgage of $100,000. This is variable so goes up and down (so far only up ☹) as the bank rate changes, but I stay 0.5% below the advertised ASB floating rate at all times.

I got 0.23% off the 2 year fixed rate so I was paying 7.42% instead of 7.65% on $165,000. When we came to end of the Fixed rate period on this, the rate was 9.4%, but I agreed the new rate when it was still 9.3% and negotiated 0.15% off that. So I'm actually paying 9.15%. The increase in the rate means I will be paying about $100 a month more on that portion of the mortgage. Ouch. On the positive side though – it is still less than it would have been if I had not sat down and talked to the banks.

I also got an agreement to refund all fees payable on my parents' and brother's New Zealand accounts, up to $20 a month on each account.

And - I got my first year Credit card fees removed, as well as the fee for joining the Credit card reward program. All in all, over the first two years, it saved us quite a packet. **Remember – if you don't ask – you don't get**!

Discount	Saving over 2 years
0.5% on Revolving Credit	765.84
0.23% On Fixed rate	557.52
Monthly Fee Refund	240.00
Parents Fee Refund	480.00
Brother's Fee Refund	480.00
Credit Card Fee Refund	110.00
Reward Scheme Refund	40.00
TOTAL SAVED	**2,673.36**

That's a whole lotta coffee. ☺

How big a reduction in fees you can get often depends on the numbers - a $265,000 mortgage is quite high (or it feels that way to me!). But my top tip, even if you aren't looking at anywhere near that much is: shop around and **talk** to the mortgage managers. I had 6 meetings with the guy at ASB; asking loads of questions about how things work in New Zealand. I also knew what I wanted to do to save money because I have read Anita Bells books on the subject a few times. ☺ I built up quite a relationship with the guy before we ever signed on the line!

If anyone is patronising, or doesn't give you the time of day, walk out and go to the next bank or even another branch of the same bank. With ANZ Bank I never got further than a first meeting with them for this reason, that and they would only give me a measly 0.1% discount on the rate and charge me $25 a month for the privilege! Westpac nearly got my banking business, except that when I was passed on to the "Personal Relationship Manager" he was utterly obnoxious! Patronising and arrogant, he spoke to me as if I was 12 years old with a piggy bank! Bear in mind at this point I was well on the way to getting my finances sorted, had budgeted till I was blue in the face and could tell exactly what I had in the bank to the cent. I was not a happy bunny. 😒 No one should treat you like an idiot – even if you do know nothing about the subject.

One thing I would suggest is to ask every bank for quotes, and ask then them all to negotiate. I rapidly took two banks off my list because they wouldn't move on rates (ANZ and HSBC). You will rapidly get to know what the deal is and get a feel for the best way to structure the mortgage.

What about paying fortnightly instead of monthly? Will it make your mortgage cheaper? Too right it will, over the life of the mortgage, if you take half of the normal monthly amount, and pay it every fortnight! We don't do this because the way we have ours set up it actually doesn't give us an advantage. With a Revolving Credit mortgage often at a higher interest rate, you need to keep all your pennies in that account as long as possible, and paying fortnightly drops the balance faster. If you don't have a Revolving Credit mortgage, fortnightly is better. And bear in mind – often in New Zealand – people get paid fortnightly rather than monthly, so it can work out really well to do this.

Make sure that it is **half the monthly payment which is paid every fortnight**. If the bank just works out a fortnightly payment – then it does not help you pay off your mortgage faster.

If you want to see this in action – I suggest you pop to the Westpac Website: www.westpac.co.nz

Under Home Loans – pick the calculators option, and then click on the Fine Tune Your Loan option. (This by the way – is the online calculator I use most for sorting out my mortgages and working out my budgets and generally playing around with numbers.)

It will show you exactly how much money you can save between a monthly mortgage and splitting the amount in half and paying that fortnightly.

- Plug in the numbers for a monthly mortgage and hit calculate.
- That tells you the monthly payments and how much interest you pay overall.
- Under Change payment frequency - click option
- [a] (half monthly amount paid fortnightly).
- Hit recalculate.
- It then tells in nice friendly red letters just how much you save overall and how much time you just knocked off your mortgage.
- If that doesn't make Mortgages interesting – nothing will.

This works because when you pay monthly – you make 12 payments a year. But when you pay fortnightly – you make 26 payments a year – not 24! So you basically force yourself to pay an extra months payment each year. Make sure that you budget for this though. What is going to happen is that in one or two months a year – you will make 3 mortgage payments instead of 2. This can hurt if you do not realize it's coming!

SHOULD I PAY OFF MY HOME LOAN AS FAST AS POSSIBLE?

Challenge the way the world works,
And work at it every day.
www.moxie.co.nz

There's a very common school of thought – particularly in New Zealand, that paying off the mortgage as fast as possible is the way to go. To be honest, I had never really thought of it myself till I came here and read that flippin' book – I just assumed that I would pay my mortgage off over 25 years and that was it! The problem with this was that I had never really appreciated just how much money you actually pay for a house when you take into account the interest payments over 25 years.

Our house cost $595,000 to buy. But that is **not** how much it will eventually cost us to **own** it! Most people forget that the eventual cost of owning your own home includes all the interest payments you have to make. Over 20 years taking just a relatively small mortgage of $265,000 (small compared to the cost of the house that is) will add a whopping $260,000 to what we have to pay to **own** the house. So it will actually have cost us $855,000 to buy!!!!! (Interestingly – if you were me anyway – by paying half the monthly amount fortnightly for the whole 20 years we would save a whopping $50,000 on the total cost of our house- that's a whole lotta coffee! (14,285 Flat Whites to be precise)). 😉

Now for the seriously insane "pay off your mortgage in five years" style budgeters – we would have saved a massive $204,000.00 in interest compared to a normal 20 year mortgage. Meaning that in the end – our house would actually only have cost us $651,000.00. Not too bad!

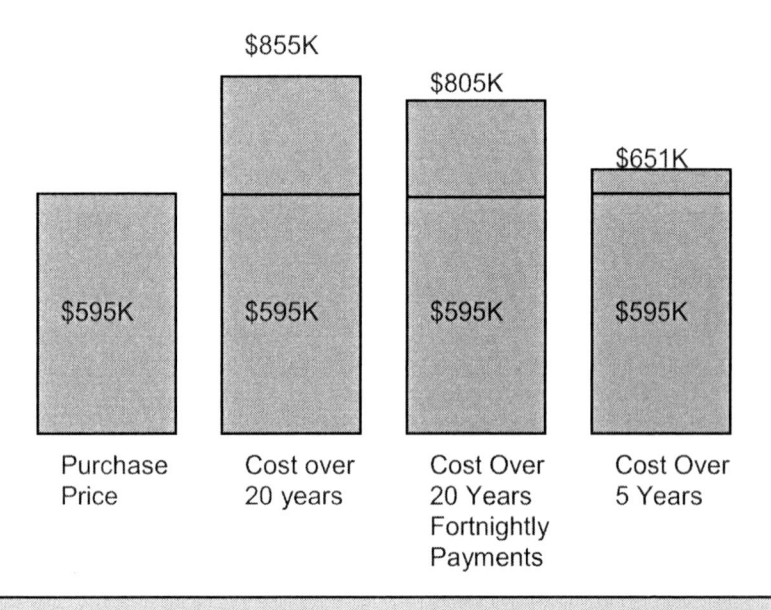

	$855K	$805K	$651K
$595K	$595K	$595K	$595K
Purchase Price	Cost over 20 years	Cost Over 20 Years Fortnightly Payments	Cost Over 5 Years

Note: This is using our original figures: $100,000 @ 8.5% over 20 years and $165,000 @ 7.42 over 20 years. Paying Fortnightly also knocks about 3 years off the length of the mortgage.

Paying your mortgage off fast and early would also mean you can live mortgage free and never have to worry about paying the bank each month. Sweet! Especially as at the moment, many people are paying well over one third of their take home pay in mortgage payments. This attitude apparently stems from the 90's when interest rates in New Zealand were over 15%, so people scrimped and scraped by to get that mortgage gone and stop having to pay it. It seems to have caught on – with many homeowners not having a mortgage at all now. Oddly this didn't seem to happen in the UK in the early 90's when interest rates also hit the same dizzying heights.

So is paying off the mortgage fast always the best thing to do? Well, this is one of those very individual things, and to be honest – it **will** be different for everyone. So as usual – there is no hard and fast rule. It really depends as far as I can see on your personal circumstances, finances, and how good you are with money. I started out with this as my main financial goal here in New Zealand and for many people it may still be the best option so I wouldn't discount it out of hand. But over time – I have decided to balance paying the mortgage off faster than normal while at the same time – investing.

You see – if you simply pay off your mortgage as fast as you can – ploughing every spare cent and then some into extra payments – where are your retirement savings? I actually heard a rather good explanation of this from the ASB advisor: if you pay off your mortgage and **only** do that, you still have no savings with which to live on, so you still have to work to earn an income to pay your bills. This includes the bills you still need to pay to be allowed to live in the home you now own – such as rates. So no retiring at the age of 40! Whereas if you were to save or invest at the same time as overpaying a bit on your mortgage you get rid of the debt earlier (and save money on interest charges) **but** you also have money set aside that you can now live on (or investments that generate an income).

I guess we all need to think about what is best for us and our families. What works for me, may not suit your needs. So its OK to decide that paying off the mortgage as rapidly as possible is your goal. But equally – you may want to pay that bit less and invest the rest. If you do want to pay off your mortgage though – do make sure you have some plan for your future income. Just remember that even if you don't have a mortgage to pay, you still need money for rates, heating, food and general living costs such as coffee.

The problem I can see with focusing solely on the mortgage is that you need to be able to pay it off fast enough so that you have time once it's paid to divert the money you were paying into creating a big pot of money to live off in retirement. Could you do it that fast? If that is what you want to do – then I really think you must read Anita Bell's book. You also need to make sure you are not going to skimp on any of your money management skills!

For us- we are aiming to have that 20-year mortgage gone in 10 years, which will still save us a healthy $142,000 – which I think we then deserve to spend on coffee. 😃

SHOULD I KEEP MONEY IN THE UK OR HAVE A SMALLER MORTGAGE IN NEW ZEALAND?

> *It's really the cat's house - we just pay the mortgage.*
> Author Unknown

What if you have a large chunk of money from a house sale back in the UK? Should you use all of that to purchase a house outright, or stick it in a UK savings account and take out a bigger mortgage in New Zealand?

Well, for a start if I had a large chunk of cash hanging around - I **would** have used it to buy the house instead of taking on a mortgage. However - there are 3 reasons that could explain at least why some people would want to take out the mortgage and keep a UK savings account;

- The existence of Revolving Credit mortgages
- You may want to invest some of the money in something other than your own home
- The exchange rate may not be good when you want to buy

Firstly – these Revolving Credit mortgages are very popular here. Some people would stick any extra savings in the revolving credit account and not pay interest on it, but still "technically" have borrowed the money from the bank. One reason for doing this would be that if you knew you were going to need that money at some point in the future, but not right now, by arranging the Revolving Credit Mortgage, you have "access to the loan", but don't pay interest on it till you use it.

Most Revolving Credit mortgages are in fact sold on the basis that you can redraw the money paid off at any time (often demonstrated as allowing you to buy a boat or a car! 😊)

The other thing that we do that goes against the "get rid of the mortgage fast" theory is that we are saving to invest alongside paying extra on the mortgage. So I can easily see that for some people it may be a good idea to use less of the proceeds from a house sale to buy your next home, and use some of it to stash away for a rainy day or in an investment. Remember that although your home is an "investment" in that it will go up in value over time – it's the one investment you can't really sell all that easily. The only way to access any money in it is to sell and buy a cheaper house or go homeless. Whereas if you put some of the funds from a UK house sale into another investment, then at some stage in the future you can sell it and access the money.

Finally, you need to bear in mind the exchange rate. It was unbelievable poor at just the time we bought our place (£1 = $2.5 😩), and in some cases it may actually be better to leave some money in the UK, pay a New Zealand mortgage and then bring the cash over when (or if) the rate improves. We made the decision that although we needed to bring almost all the money over to afford the house, we could afford to leave a small amount in the UK until we could get a better rate. We worked out that if the exchange rate £-$ went up to 2.85, it would be worth us leaving money in the UK for up to 2 years, and paying a mortgage. Bringing it over then, we would make more money on the increase in the rate than we would have spent on the extra mortgage. It's a bit "maths intensive" but you can work it out. Let's say you are considering holding back £10,000 in the UK, because the exchange rate is so bad.

- £10,000 @ $2.5   = $25,000

You now need to work out the interest that you have to pay on the extra mortgage over a year and see what that comes to:

- $25,000 @ 8.5%   = $2,125 per year

You also need to take into account the amount of money you would earn in interest on the money in the UK. At the time we bought our house, we were getting 5.25% on our UK savings. You will be able to exchange this extra money as well.

- £10,000 @ 5.2%   =   £520

Now you need to know at which rate you would need to exchange at to give you more money than you have spent on the extra mortgage interest.

- $25,000 + $2,125   = $27,125
- Divide the total you need by the amount you now have in £UK
- $27,125.00 / £10,520.00 =   **2.5784**

So in this case – the rate needs to hit £1: $2.5784 within the first year to make it worth you holding the £10,000.00 back in the UK. So you can see that really, the rate doesn't have to go up that much, for it to be worth you waiting.

To be honest – I really think it's only worth taking out a bigger mortgage if you want to wait for the exchange rate to change. It's just a personal thing – but I really don't like having a mortgage over my home, so I would rather use whatever funds I can to buy the house and not have to owe the bank so much money. But hey, many people migrating here have much bigger funds available than we had, or actually bought a cheaper house than we did, or just have a different way of looking at housing and mortgages.

Be guided by what suits you best, and if you feel you want to hold money back – that's fine. You now know that at least you can look at the costs involved.

WHAT ON EARTH IS A REVOLVING CREDIT MORTGAGE?

*Where large sums of money are concerned,
it is advisable to trust nobody.*
Agatha Christie

These are sometimes called Line Of Credit (LOC) mortgages, and are very common here in New Zealand. They are most like the Virgin One Account in the UK, in that it's a mortgage and current account rolled into one. Basically it's a current account with a whopping great overdraft. The benefit is that if you pay your salary directly into it, it reduces the amount of interest you pay on the loan. That's because you only get charged interest on the amount you are **actually** overdrawn by. They can be really good news if you save up for things like bills and Christmas, because those funds just sit in the Revolving Credit and again – you save on interest!

Bear in mind that these days, interest on your loan (or savings for that matter) is worked out every day, rather than monthly which is the way it used to be done. So if you can drop the balance of the loan by $1,000 for one day, then that day, you pay $1,000 worth of interest less. If you were to pay a $5,000 salary in, then you pay $5,000 worth of interest less, for every day you can keep that money in there. Even better, if you don't actually spend all of your salary, then the next month you pay even less interest again.

However there are some serious downsides to a Revolving Credit account, especially if you are not so good at looking after your money. They are notorious for not getting paid off, as it's all too easy to keep dipping into for buying cars, boats, shoes or coffee. The banks love them, which means as customers of the banks we really should view them with a healthy dose of suspicion. This is because unlike with a normal mortgage, you don't actually make payments to the bank. All that happens is each month; they charge any interest directly onto that account. The bank never takes any money off you to pay down the loan. You actually have to find some way of paying it off yourself – which I will cover in the next chapter!

Also, because they are usually a few % more expensive than fixed rate mortgages – you need to have a certain amount in there at all times to offset the higher interest rate. There's actually a calculation you can do to work out how much of a balance you need to keep in there to make it worthwhile (I'll put that in a later chapter). If you cannot do that – your Revolving Credit mortgage is going to cost you **more** in interest each month than if you had a normal mortgage. That is bad. You also need to take into account that your normal Fixed Rate mortgage won't have a fee on it every month, whereas your Revolving Credit mortgage is highly likely to have fees attached to it. Think very carefully about whether you really will save money. Just because the bank tells you that you will it doesn't mean it's written in stone that you actually will.

I would say if you are thinking of a Revolving Credit account you do need to be **very good** with organising your money, as it's all too easy to end up with the overdraft limit never going down and you never pay off that part of the mortgage. Some banks have Revolving Credit mortgages that automatically drop the overdraft limit each month, so if you want a Revolving Credit but feel concerned about your ability to pay the loan off, then look for those. ASB for example has Orbit, which is their normal revolving credit account, and Orbit Fastrack, which has a reducing overdraft limit.

The cynic in me would dearly like to know; if Revolving Credit accounts allow you to pay off your mortgage faster; why do banks offer a "Fastrack" Revolving Credit? Perhaps because the banks know full well that in the vast majority of cases, people do not pay off their mortgages at all with Revolving Credit, let alone faster?

You also really do need to be able to use a credit card if you choose a Revolving Credit mortgage. By putting as many of your monthly expenses on the credit card as possible, you keep the balance in the revolving credit account as high as possible for as long as possible (or the overdraft as low as possible – depending on how you want to look at it). I.e.: your wages stay in the Revolving Credit for as much of the month as you can manage. You really don't want to spend a cent out of your wages until the day before you get paid again if you can help it. However you must **always** make sure you know exactly how much you can spend on the credit card without getting into trouble. For this to work, and not get you into debt you **must** be able to pay off the Credit Card each month in full. If you don't think you can do that then it may not be a good idea to have this kind of mortgage. Do not use the Credit Card for buying items that you do not have the money for. That way lies ever-increasing mortgage debt. Maybe just have a very small limit on the credit card. You need the equivalent of 2 months spending as a minimum limit.

Be very wary once you get here of any company offering to save you lots of money by re-organising your mortgage and showing you how to pay less interest. They are talking about changing you from a normal mortgage to a Revolving Credit. Some companies I hear of are even charging customers up front to "analyse" the situation and tell them if they can save money, and then charge them for setting it up. Run away. A normal mortgage broker or even the banks can do it all for you for free. There is no magic involved in saving money by using a Revolving Credit mortgage; just a bit of work in keeping your spending under control and managing your finances properly.

A new addition to the Kiwi "Mortgage Market" is an Offset mortgage like First Direct or Woolwich do in the UK, where you can have different accounts that are all rolled into one for the purposes of working out the interest. BNZ (Bank of New Zealand) have recently released "Total Money". You can have up to 10 accounts (with a Non Negotiable charge of $10 a month for all of them☺.) This has all the advantages of a Revolving Credit mortgage in that it cuts the interest bill, but also allows you to keep your current account separate, as well as having separate savings accounts, so at all times you know how much money you have available and how much you have paid off your home loan.

What's more, in this particular bank's set up – you can actually combine accounts for other family members. So you have separate accounts for you and your partner, and even your parents. This is being sold as "do your parents have a chunk of spare cash they want to be kind enough to let you use to reduce your mortgage costs?" Bear in mind that if they do that – they won't earn any interest on their money. Nice if you can get it! In fact – we do something similar. My mum has given me a chunk of their cash (the proceeds from their UK house sale that they didn't use to buy the New Zealand house) – which they will be living off at some point. That sits in my Revolving

Credit account – which means I don't pay 10.25% on that amount. However as I wouldn't be comfortable with my mum and dad not getting any interest, and they really need it paid anyway; each month I work out how much money they would have earned in interest if it was in a savings account – and pay that into the "savings pot". (Remember the interest on savings is lower than interest on lending.) I guess if nothing else – it shows that you can be flexible about how you arrange your finances – you don't always have to do it the way the banks want you to! ☺

Now the way this works: say you have $100,000 in a mortgage. That's account 1. Now you have a joint cheque account that your pay goes into, let's say $5,000 a month, that's account 2. And let's say you have $10,000 in savings – that's account 3. Interest is charged on the "overall balance", not the $100,000 owed in the mortgage.

Mortgage Account 1	-100,000
Cheque Account 2	5,000
Savings Account 3	10,000
Overall balance	**-85,000**

So you only get charged interest on the $85,000. Over time that makes a pretty hefty difference.

This is exactly the same way that a Revolving Credit mortgage works, except in that case you don't have different accounts, so it's hard to see what is savings, versus what is mortgage, versus what is your monthly income. I'm a huge fan of this type of account (but then it's the type of mortgage I had with First Direct in the UK, only they didn't charge me every month for the privilege!) In fact the only reason I haven't changed from ASB to BNZ is because when I went into the bank to ask about it the guy I spoke to wasn't in the least bit interested in talking to me. I was actually way more excited by the whole thing than he was. I made a decision to stick with ASB because my Personal Relationship Manager is a great bloke, and I'm actually managing the Orbit facility well anyway with the help of Quicken and a weirdly organisied mind.

HOW DO I ACTUALLY PAY OFF A REVOLVING CREDIT MORTGAGE?

"Mortgage: a house with a guilty conscience"
Anon

So, if all this mortgage is, is a whopping great overdraft, and you never actually have to make a payment to the bank to pay down the loan: how exactly **do** you ever pay it off?

You need to have a way of setting aside some money each month that will be used to pay down the mortgage eventually. If you ever had an endowment mortgage in the UK, then think of it the same way. In that case; you only ever paid interest to the bank, but you had to put some money aside into the Endowment in order (hopefully) to pay off the mortgage at the end of the day. In this case, you need to put that money into some savings, and keep it sitting inside the Revolving Credit account (so you don't pay interest on it!).

With me so far?

Well, I have found that the best way for me to do it is to use Quicken's "Savings Pots". It doesn't matter two hoots what you use, as long as you know that those funds are destined to pay off your mortgage and are **not for spending**. I have a savings pot set up called "Principle Payments". I know that if I had a normal mortgage of $100,000 with a rate of 10.25%, then I would be paying a total of $981 to the bank each month. My interest for the month is around $300 because I have funds sitting in the revolving credit, so I pay $681 into the savings pot.

To find the savings pots in Quicken (because for some reason they are not obvious):

- From the Home Page
- Click on Features in the task bar at the top.
- In the drop-down menu, click on Planning.
- Then Click on Savings Goals
- Then Click on New to set up a new savings pot.

To make this easier to see – because I realize this is hard to understand unless you have a copy of Quicken in front of you: we will assume that we get paid $6,000 a month, and that we pay $1,000 in "mortgage" payments. That leaves us with $5,000 a month we can spend. The $1,000 gets transferred into the savings pot, in Quicken, but as far as the bank is concerned; it's just sitting in the Revolving Credit account. So at the end of the month, when you next get paid, if you had spent all of the $5,000, the bank still shows the $1,000 sitting there, and that you are only $99,000 overdrawn on the account. Quicken shows that you set aside the $1,000, and shows that you are still $100,000 overdrawn, and now have $1,000 in the savings pot. Do the same thing the next month, and the bank says you are only overdrawn by $98,000; and Quicken says you are still overdrawn by $100,000 but now have $2,000 set aside in the savings pot.

Month	Starting Bank Balance	Wages Paid In	New Bank Balance	Save to Savings pot	Money spent	Cumulative Savings	Ending Bank balance	Ending Quicken Balance
1	100,000	6,000	94,000	1,000	5,000	1,000	**99,000**	100,000
2	99,000	6,000	93,000	1,000	5,000	2,000	**98,000**	100,000
3	98,000	6,000	92,000	1,000	5,000	3,000	**97,000**	100,000
4	97,000	6,000	91,000	1,000	5,000	4,000	**96,000**	100,000
5	96,000	6,000	90,000	1,000	5,000	5,000	**95,000**	100,000

Now because I really want to pay off the mortgage, every so often I actually ask the bank to reduce the overdraft limit. When I have saved up $5,000 in that savings pot, I ask the bank to reduce the limit by $5,000, and then in my Quicken accounts, all I do is transfer the money from the "savings pot" back into my Revolving Credit account on Quicken.

Month	Starting Bank Balance	Wages paid in	New Bank Balance	Save to Savings pot	Money spent	Cumulative Savings	Ending Bank balance	Ending Quicken Balance
5	95,000	-	95,000	-5,000	-	0.00	95,000	**95,000**

My Quicken file now says I am $95,000 overdrawn: there is no change in the banks balance - so all you have to do is ask them to drop the limit to $95,000. You have now locked in all those savings, and actually paid down $5,000 of your mortgage. Time for a celebratory cup of coffee I think.

This is just one way of using a Revolving Credit account. I have a large overdraft limit because I figured that I would actually have a large amount of savings that I could use to lower the interest I pay. Some months I actually pay no interest at all on it. If you do not think you will have that much in savings, then you could always have a much smaller limit, even the equivalent of your monthly pay cheque.

As an alternative to saving your mortgage payments in $5,000 chunks, you could always determine an amount you want to pay down each month, and ask the bank each month to drop your overdraft limit by that amount once you get paid. That way – you simply cannot spend all of the money you get paid.

However you choose to use the Revolving Credit – work out a method that suits you to make sure you pay off the balance. Do not get caught out like so many people: with a mortgage that never gets paid off.

WHAT BALANCE DO I NEED IN THIS REVOLVING CREDIT ACCOUNT?

*"Maths is like love
- a simple idea but it can get complicated."*
Anon.

Sorry – this involves some (more) maths.☹

This tells you how much money you need to have in a Revolving Credit account so that it doesn't cost you more in interest each month than a fixed rate account. That's because the Revolving Credit interest rate is usually higher than the fixed rate.

(Using my original mortgage numbers as an example)

STEP 1
Divide the Fixed Rate by the Revolving Credit rate
7.42 ÷ 9.05 = 0.8198

STEP 2
Turn that into a %
0.8198 x 100 = 81.98 %

STEP 3
Take that away from 100%
100% - 81.98% = 18.02%

STEP 4
Work out 18.02% of your total Revolving Credit Overdraft Limit.
18.02% of $100,000 = $18,020

RESULT
I need to keep $18,020 cash in the account at all times to outweigh the higher interest rate.

This means that although I am allowed to be overdrawn by $100,000, I need to make sure I'm never overdrawn by more than $81,980. If I don't have the $18,020 to stick in the account, then I'm better off with a fixed rate loan. More importantly – if I had more cash than that in savings that I could keep in the account, it will be saving me interest.

This was taken from a post on the www.propertytalk.co.nz forum.

BUYING YOUR NEW ZEALAND HOME

The fellow that owns his own home is always just coming out of a hardware store.
Frank McKinney Hubbard

It takes hands to build a house, but only hearts can build a home
Author Unknown

*A perfect summer day is when
the sun is shining,
the breeze is blowing,
the birds are singing,
and the lawn mower is broken.*
James Dent

*One only needs two things in life:
WD-40 to make things go,
and duct tape to make them stop.*
G.M. Weilacher

IS IT REALLY MUCH EASIER TO BUY A HOUSE IN NEW ZEALAND?

> *"In a real estate man's eye,
> the most expensive part of the city is
> where he has a house to sell"*
> Will Rogers

Many people find the whole process of buying and selling houses here a lot easier than back in the UK. In many ways it is but you still need to be **very** careful. Estate Agents here are not angels and they are just as likely to try pulling a fast one as an agent in the UK. Especially once they know (or think) you are a "filthy rich migrant" (and trust me – they will! It's like we have this big pink flashing neon sign stuck above our heads or something – like a British accent.☺)

The problem is, compared to the UK process; the New Zealand system **looks** dead easy. In the UK you can be waiting round for months for an offer on your house to go through, to find that the day before you exchange, the buyers inform you that they really couldn't ever afford your home in the first place. In New Zealand, once both parties have agreed on an offer, and signed the "Sale and Purchase Agreement" (S&P), you have a set amount of time to exchange (it's called "Going Unconditional" here), which is often only a few weeks. You then also have a set amount of time to "settle" – which is like completion in the UK. Again that is often only a few weeks.

You as the buyer of a property are usually responsible for getting the S&P agreement drawn up. You can ask the agent to write it up for you, but you **must** get your lawyer to check it before you sign it. The S&P agreement contains:

- Your name(s) and the sellers name
- The address of the property and legal description of it (that's just a bunch of codes the council uses; the selling agent will have all that.)
- The price you want to pay
- The deposit you want to pay
- When you want to settle (complete)
- The interest rate you will pay to the seller if you do not settle on time
- Any "chattels" the property comes with (cooker, spa pool, flash car etc.)
- Contact details for the buyer, seller and their lawyers.
- Any conditions that need to be met before the sale becomes unconditional (exchange).

Once you have drawn that up: it is taken to the seller by the estate agent. The seller can do a few things with it. Firstly – they can laugh at your offer and refuse it (often they get "insulted" that you didn't offer enough 😳). They can ask the agent to come back to you and get you to pay more. Or, they can write in a counter-offer. With a counter offer basically they cross out anything they don't like, and put in what they want instead. The other important thing the seller does is to sign the agreement, and initial any changes. At that point you are negotiating, and the poor old S&P gets pushed from pillar to post, with crossing outs, and extra signatures all over the place. Personally – I think it's a silly system, because it can get very difficult to read the changes after a few goes. You end up having to write things smaller and smaller to get it in. I think it would be much easier to verbally negotiate and **then** draw up the agreement, but ho hum.

The conditions you put in allow you as a buyer to check the property out before committing to buying – things such as finance, builder's reports, valuation and checking that a motorway isn't going to be ploughed through the bathroom. The seller can also insert conditions if they want: often they don't but you may find a "Cash-out Clause" gets put in. This allows the seller to keep marketing the property, and accept a higher offer if one comes along. If they don't put that in there, you cannot be gazzumped. Even if a better offer **is** made, the cash-out clause allows you 3 days grace to "Go Unconditional" (exchange) before losing out.

Once signed by both parties and dated, the S&P agreement is binding. So the buyer can't back out for any old reason, and the seller can't accept another offer just because someone else is sniffing round your dream home. The only way for either party to back out of the agreement is if the conditions are not satisfied; perhaps one of the reports you got showed that indeed; there is a 6-lane motorway being built outside (not too likely in New Zealand, but you get the picture.)

> Get your solicitor to check that you will be able to get insurance on your home. Some homes built pre-1935 are hard to get insured in some instances, and occasionally companies won't insure houses in particularly earthquake prone areas or in some coastal areas.

Often, you "go unconditional" within a few weeks at the most – at which point both parties are committed to selling and buying. A few short weeks after that: you own a new house. Added to the simplicity of this; you often find agents will bend over backwards to help you out: taking you round the properties; drawing up the agreements; finding you a solicitor; valuer; builder – anything you need to get that sale done. It all seems so easy compared to the weeks and months of teeth gnashing and nail biting in the UK, where it can all fall to pieces at the last minute. 😊

But is it really that simple?

Hell no. Just because you have moved to New Zealand – it doesn't mean estate agents are automatically cute and cuddly. If you are distrustful of agents in the UK, you should be here too. Neil Jenman's "Don't Sign Anything!" is a really good book and explains a lot of the nasty tricks that agents can pull. It's a bit of a scary read but I figure forewarned is forearmed and it's good to know when you are about to be sold a lemon! It's especially good at talking you through the auction process and what to watch for.
www.jenman.com.au

My main advice is literally "Don't sign anything" not without a solicitor looking it over. You wouldn't do it in the UK, so don't do it here. **Always** get your solicitor to check the Sale & Purchase agreement before you sign it. The estate agent often draws up the contract and they are less than trustworthy most of the time. They work for the seller, not for you. If you don't understand something ask your **solicitor** and not the agent. The solicitor works for you, and will give you the advice that works in your interest.

> I have just had a situation where I drew up a Sale & Purchase agreement and presented it to a local agent. The agent wanted to rewrite it onto their "Own Agreement": the same document with their logo splashed all over it.
>
> Well, I went in to pick up the agreement to find that they had altered everything except the price. They had changed the deposit (I "had to pay" $9000 because that's their commission – yeah right!) They changed the interest rate for late settlement (they usually put in 14% - but it can be anything), they changed the date of settlement, and most importantly – they changed every single one of the conditions I had written in. In fact – I'm really not sure why they didn't add a few extra thousand onto the price while they were at it!
>
> Then they tried to fob me off by telling me it had simply been changed into "Estate Agent Speak". Load of old cobblers! ☺ It's just not true. An agent has no right to try and pull that kind of stunt – it's unethical, it's unprofessional – and it's not entirely legal because it meant they were not presenting my offer to the seller, which they are obliged to do by law.
>
> It's worth noting that at this point: I'm buying rental properties in New Zealand, so am confident and able to write my own agreements and they have clauses in which mean I can pull out later if my solicitor doesn't like what I've done.
>
> **Do not write your own S&P agreements** unless you have had some education on the subject. As a new migrant – do **not** get forced into signing anything without your solicitor looking it over first. Because as I explained to that agent – there's no way our solicitor would have fallen for that load of guff!

Also, be warned that if you write anything on any piece of paper that has some basic details on it and a price and you sign it – it can be used as an offer. Offers do **not** need to be written on the standard Sale and Purchase agreement forms (which are produced by the Auckland District Law Society). I have had an agent write down what we discussed as a potential price for a house and ask me to sign it. Apparently – I really did look that stupid! 😳 I told them to get stuffed! Signing that piece of paper would have potentially committed me to buying a house I really wasn't that interested in, especially as she neglected to write down any conditions😠. Be **very** careful.

Be extremely wary of anyone that the agents recommend to you. Whether it's solicitors, mortgage brokers, valuers, builders, chief-cook-and-bottle-washers or Uncle Tom Cobbley and all. You can never be sure that they are not paying "commissions" to the agent, so they are not truly independent. If you are not the only one paying them, then they are not working for you. If in doubt, you can ask the estate agent if they are receiving commissions from anyone they recommend to you. They are obliged by law to "fess up" if you ask them outright. If you do not ask, they do not need to tell you.😝

You should always get a full builders report and valuation done. New Zealand houses are just built differently than in the UK (insulation is a "new fangled" idea,) and it helps to get a good idea of exactly what type of building you are buying. You may get a surprise! You also need to be aware of "Leaky Building Syndrome" where some modern houses are not watertight. That's a bit of an issue.😨 I want to know of any problems before I buy just to make sure I'm really not buying a lemon. You also need to get a Land Information Memorandum (LIM) report done. This is a report from the local council that confirms whether all the necessary permits and consents have been obtained and filed. You will need to have listed in your conditions of purchase that you wish to get these reports and that buying the property is conditional on the reports being satisfactory.

A builders report (like a survey in the UK) will cost around $400 - $600. Now that may sound like a lot, but hey – you are about to spend around $350,000 on a house! (The average price of a house in New Zealand by the end of 2007). Paying $600 to check the house isn't going to fall down is not a lot of money. I use a company called Realsure for my building reports. They are easy and friendly to deal with, and have a habit of getting a copy of the report to me by email on the same day that they actually inspect the house.
www.realsure.co.nz

A LIM report will cost about $150 - $250. Some councils will let you look at the files they have for the property you are interested in, so you can save money by doing that and just paying the council to photocopy any bits you want to keep.

Deposits are "usually" 10%, but you can offer a lesser one if you want. That would go in the S&P agreement as well. We gave a 5% deposit because we were buying an expensive house and 10% was a fair whack of money. Bear in mind, unlike in the UK, deposits are paid to the estate agent, not to the solicitors because they want to be sure they get their mitts on their commission before anything else! I have come across Kiwis that think we are mad in the UK to trust our solicitors with the deposit money whereas I find it completely bizarre that you would give **any** money to an estate agent for "safekeeping". You can pay whatever you deem suitable for the deposit if the seller agrees to it. The agent will often tell you it has to be a certain amount, which again – is a load of cobblers. The Sale & Purchase agreement is a contract between you and the seller, and if you agree to a $5 deposit, it's not up to the agent to refuse it.

When you have the S&P drawn up, it's fairly standard to have a condition in there that says "Subject to finance". Basically it means if you can't get a mortgage, you don't have to go through with the purchase. Just be aware that it should actually read "Subject to finance satisfactory to the purchaser". This can avoid you being forced to take a mortgage out that is going to cost you more than it should including sometimes being forced to borrow off the seller at very high interest rates (no - I'm not kidding.)

My best advice is:

(A) Not to rush into anything and do lots of research.
Talk to as many people as you can who know the areas you are looking at. It may look great but is it? You need to find out what the specific concerns are in each area, especially any sunlight issues, because if the sun doesn't get onto your property for part of the day or even year, you are going to be **very** cold! (This is a big problem in Wellington for Eastbourne, Seatoun, and the Eastern Bays for example.)

I know it's often tempting to want to buy straight away and get settled; but my heartfelt feeling is that you will actually settle a lot easier if you make sure that the house you buy is the **right** one for you and your family – and that can take time. No matter how long you spend researching, nothing quite beats being on the ground to make these decisions.

Where we ended up – in the Wairarapa – is so utterly different from where we wanted to go to start with (Eastbourne in Wellington or the Kapiti Coast). But taking the time to really explore – showed us that this was the place for us – and we are now blissfully happy that we did move here!

(B) Get a valuation on any property you are interested in.

It will cost a few hundred bucks (we have just paid $450 for one) - but it tells you what it's really worth - from someone who works for you not the seller or the agent. Most of the online valuations available (such as from Quotable Value) actually show the Ratings Valuations and **not** the market value of a property.

Quotable Value will give you estimates, but without organising a special valuation with them, it's not really worth much because they don't visit the property or the area. QV supply a range of reports that you buy, costing from a couple of dollars to about $70, and they will sell you lists of comparative sales. But it's the same information as you can find on Help Sell My Property for free (www.helpsellmyproperty.co.nz). And none of those options are as good as a proper registered valuation.

(C) Don't use companies recommended by an estate agent.

They may be paying "Commission" to the agent and are therefore **not** independent. I always take a card from the agent for the companies they recommend, and then I know who not to call. If you do choose to use someone recommend by the agent; ask the agent if they are getting commissions from them.

(D) Check out some auctions and see what happens.

Watch out for "Vendor bids" where the agent bids the price up on behalf of the Vendor. It's totally legal to do that here. We went to one auction where we had been told the house was expected to go for "top 400's". The bidding started at $600,000. (Never trust the number you are given by the agent either!) There was only one guy bidding (and lots of interested watchers like me). He bid against the agent only and ended up paying $780,000. I cannot for the life of me work out why he didn't just stop. But ho hum not my money. Incidentally, in auctions, if the property doesn't reach the reserve, and you are the highest "under bidder" – you have the right to go into one on one negotiation with the seller. You can actually end up bidding against someone else for the "right to negotiate with the seller".

Bear in mind that, as in the UK, if you win a property auction: it is an unconditional sale. Make sure you have done all your homework if you want to buy at auction, and make sure you have the money to buy it.

(E) Do not assume that New Zealand estate agents are any better than UK agents.

I have now dealt with an awful lot of estate agents here in New Zealand. Most of them are fine, and no problem at all to deal with. A few are really very good, and wouldn't dream of doing anything vaguely dodgy. Some wouldn't dream of doing anything that **isn't** dodgy. Some are just downright incompetent. Just like in the UK.

It's worth bearing in mind that most agents or salespeople are only paid commission; they do not get a salary. This puts them in the position of having to get sales through; otherwise they go hungry. This can lead to unethical behaviour.

WHAT'S ALL THIS BBO & BEO NONSENSE ON HOUSE ADVERTS?

Advertising is legalized lying.
H. G. Wells

This is a real "pet peeve" of mine! You are in the UK, dreaming about your new life, and of course; you go house hunting on the Internet. You find a mansion on the beach front – with a pool and Jacuzzi, - an "Entertainers delight" it says. (Get used to cringe-worthy cheesy real estate ads!) So you look to see if it's in your price range. Well? Is it? Ummm. I can't find the bit that says what the price is! This, more than anything else about the New Zealand housing market, drives me bonkers.

Many properties don't have any prices on them. In that case all you really have to go on is the GV/RV (Government or Rating Valuation). That's the value on which the rates are worked out. Which remember, has absolutely nothing at all to do with the price or market value of the house, or what you will end up paying for it. So basically – a complete waste of ink.

Anyway – when drooling over the property websites, you will find that where the price would be in a UK property advert, you get the following options:

Auction
A public sale of property in which prospective purchasers bid until the highest price is reached (or not as the case often is). For a discussion on that – it's back to Neil Jenman's "Don't

sign anything!" You could ask the agent for a guide price, but it will probably be nothing at all like the price the seller is expecting, or would accept.

BBO / BEO
Buyer Budget Over or Buyer Enquiry Over
This is "sort of" a guide but as with a lot of this – often nothing like what the seller actually wants. Apparently it means you have to offer more than that number – but hey – it's not carved in stone ☺ I personally read this as the asking price just as I would in the UK, and offer below it. So far it tends to work!

> In late 2007, an estate agent in Wellington was taken to court and found guilty of misconduct for advertising a property with a BBO of $380,000 when the sellers had stated that they would not take less than $410,000. The court found that agents should now ensure that the BBO or BEO **has** to reflect a price near to that which the vendor would accept. The judge ruled that a BBO or BEO is an actual price!

MWP
Marketed Without Price ☺
Truly - the most ridiculously unhelpful bit of advertising nonsense I have **ever** seen. I mean – why bother? In fact; I was once told by an agent who had put this on a property that he had done so because "He couldn't possibly put a price on the house". Ok: let me get this straight – you spend all day every day marketing properties and selling them to people, and yet – you have no idea what any given property is worth???? Can you imagine pulling that one on **your** boss???? The mind boggles!

PBN
Price by Negotiation
I'm sure that works best over coffee and cake, unfortunately – you hardly ever negotiate directly with the seller, instead it's through the agent. I always thought this was daft. And besides – what's the chance of negotiating a mansion down to ten bucks and a flock of sheep????

In fact we recently did put an offer in on a house that was listed as PBN. Normally I don't touch anything without a price; but this house had been on sale about 3 months previously with a price, and then taken off the market. So we drew up an offer, based on the previous asking price. The seller wouldn't countersign the offer. Which means that she wasn't going to negotiate. So why on **earth** advertise as a Price By Negotiation

POA
Price on Application
Always says to me "overpriced" but that's just me! And besides – just try "applying" for the price and see what an unhelpful response you get – back to MWP as often as not! Or you get this really strange "Low, Mid or High 200's, 300's or 1.5millions's – I'm not sure what on earth to make of that! Sometimes – I think what this actually means is "Think of a number and triple it!" It sure never seems to mean, "think of a number and halve it."

Tender
Make a formal written offer for a property by a set date.
You will generally be given a "Tender Document" laying out all the terms and conditions – but it's up to you whether you fill that in or just put a normal offer together. I personally don't go near "tenders". They are basically Dutch Auctions, and way too stressful because they are often used as a way of the agents

playing two potential purchasers against each other to get the price up. It's more honest to just run an auction.

GV / RV
Government or Rating Valuation.
Sometimes seen as Capital valuation as well – just to confuse the issue!
Well yeah, but how does that help? It may have been from 2-3 years ago. Ratings Valuations are generally done by QV (Quotable Value), and they are done every 2-3 years in some areas – every year in others – it's worth remembering that no one from QV actually goes to look at all these properties, and that this is **not** the market value of a property.

And this **still** doesn't tell you how much people want for the place. It's not a useful guide in any way. You just try telling the agent you want to pay the GV for a property because that's the price – and see the look of horror march across their face!

I think it's worth asking the agent up front if RV means it's a Registered Valuation or a Rating Valuation. If nowt else; it tells that agent that you know a thing or two. Of course you may get an agent that didn't know there was a difference in the first place!

A Set Price
E.g.: $350,000
Ta da! Just like in the UK. You see a picture – and it has a number by it! Genius idea and my preferred option. It tells you just what you need to know and I've noticed you often get this with lower priced properties.

If the ad says tender or auction your only way of getting a guide price of what the seller wants is to phone the agent and try and get a number out of them. I found that this was in no way helpful, even if they did tell you a number. Often they are trying to just get your interest with a silly low number which the seller would never accept and is often nothing like what the agent told the seller the house was worth.

That's why we got a valuation before we made an offer on our house. This place was advertised with a price (I stopped going to see houses without prices – just too much time wasted). They wanted $650,000, but the valuation came in at $606,000. So we knew ahead of time that if we could get it at that price, we would not be overpaying. We got it for $595,000 in the end.

Multi Offers.

If you have put an offer in on a property, and it was lower than the seller wanted; you may be told by the estate agent that there is another offer on the table and you need to increase your offer. If this happens; ask the agent for a form to fill in to go with your new offer. This form states that your offer is your best and final offer. The other party should sign one too, and you can ask to see a copy of their form (it wont have any details of the offer on it).

If you **do** ask to see the form, you often find that the second offer, "mysteriously disappears" ☻. Don't re-do your offer unless you have to fill in a form stating it's your best and final one!

HOW DO I FIND OUT HOW MUCH TO PAY FOR A HOUSE?

"If you've been aggressively marketing your property for six weeks and if you don't have a bloated dead cow in your front yard, your house is probably priced 10 percent over fair market value."
Ray Brown

You can get a lot of useful info from websites such as QV (Quotable Value) and Terranet on local values.
https://www.qv.co.nz
https://www.terranet.co.nz

I think it's worth paying for a proper valuation to be done especially if you are buying fairly quickly after arriving in the country. In New Zealand you will often see house values quoted in so many different ways: GV, CV, QV, RV: It's mind boggling. Even born and bred Kiwis don't understand the difference half the time. So here is a potted run down:

QV: Quotable Value
Quotable Value is the company that values property for the councils so they know how much to charge in rates. If you see a QV value, or you buy a valuation off their website, what you get is the Ratings Valuation (RV). I think it's important to know that Quotable Value don't actually ever visit the properties they value.

RV (1): Ratable Valuation
The value the council uses to bill you for your rates.

CV: Capital Value
This is exactly the same as the Rateable Value above; it's just that someone obviously thought it would be a good idea to make the whole thing truly complicated. The CV is made up of 2 things: The Land Value, plus the Improvements Value (that is: the house that was built on the land)

GV: Government Valuation
Exactly the same as QV, RV and CV. Why on earth do we need four different names for the same thing? No wonder people are confused.

RV (2): Registered Valuation
(Just to confuse the issue even further)
This is a valuation obtained by a Registered Valuer, which they based on the selling price of several similar properties in the area. This gives you a reasonable idea of the actual Market Value of a property, and is ideally what you want.

Market Value
What the property should actually sell for. The best way to find this out is to get a Registered Valuation, which looks at sales of comparable properties.
The QV, CV and RV(1) valuations have nowt to do with the market value of a property, and the price you will be paying.

One of the best ways to get a feel for property values is to do the legwork yourself. Thankfully Open Homes are a local pastime here, and you can whiz round several homes on a Sunday in an area you are looking at and get a feel for what you like and how much they are asking for.

QV provides a whole range of reports that you can download for any given property. The best one is the E-Valuer, which will cost $39.95. This provides an estimated "value", recommended selling range, sales history (which tells you what the seller actually paid for it – I find that really interesting), and some recent comparable sales. This is a really good start when you find a property you like – but I would suggest that you don't necessarily rely too heavily on the **estimated** valuation or selling range. QV still don't visit the house, so it's all a bit "wet-finger-in-the-wind" when it comes to accuracy. The other interesting thing that QV provides: you can download a Demographic Profile of the area. This is similar to the UK's "Up My Street", and tells you the average age of residents in the area, their ethnicity, employment status, income, housing status. It gives you a snapshot of the area you are interesting in. This one is free – even better.

You can also find out what properties in your chosen area sold for by going to a website called Help Sell My property: www.helpsellmyproperty.co.nz

This is run by Harcourts estate agents, but carries the actual price that all houses sell for, whether sold by Harcourts or not. It can take a few weeks to a few months for the information to be updated, but it is well worth keeping an eye on the site. I prefer this site to the Quotable Value website; its easier to use, easier to read, and its free ☺.

WHAT ABOUT YOUR FUTURE FINANCES?

> *I've never met you, but thanks to statistics, one of the things I can say about you with a reasonable degree of certainty is that so far you have done stuff all about saving voluntarily for your retirement.*
> Gareth Morgan
> Pension Panic

What are the chances that there will be any sort of state pension for us when we finally stop working? It's not looking good – whether you are talking about the UK or New Zealand. And if we do by some miracle, get one, what are the chances that we could actually live on it? That is looking even grimmer. So whether we like it or not, it really is going to be up to us to make sure we have enough money to retire, and live comfortably. Many people are struggling to save anything out of their salaries here in New Zealand, so it pays to think very carefully about how you want to deal with this.

Please do not put it off. Living on a low salary is one thing when you are young and more able to cope with financial hardship. It's quite another when you can no longer work to earn an income.

Investing for a future is an area that I've personally experienced a big difference in from being in the UK. I've honestly been bowled over by the sheer opportunity available here to invest in a future. In fact there is an entire industry in New Zealand, devoted to wealth creation; something I was certainly never aware of in the UK. This is usually outside what I guess would be considered normal in the UK. Many more people "do their own thing" rather than relying on a "pension scheme". Many Kiwis are not happy to just let the future happen to them, and go out there and **make** it happen. I know many people who do this despite very low incomes, and no degree level education. So it can be done ☺

The main principle of investing for a future is:

PAY YOURSELF FIRST

or

SAVE FIRST – SPEND SECOND.

HOW DO I SAVE AND INVEST ENOUGH TO RETIRE ON?

> *I advise that you take the wisdom of Algamish*
> *and say to yourselves,*
> *"A part of all I earn is mine to keep."*
> George Clason,
> The Richest Man in Babylon

So, how do you do it? Well, the **"Pay Yourself First"** principle is the main thing to get your head round. Unfortunately for many of us, it's the first stumbling block. Almost all of us firmly believe that we cannot afford to save the money, when we have to work so hard to make our salaries last the month in the first place. So you probably don't want to hear that you should set aside **10%** of your pay **before** you spend any of it! 😂 If that is exactly your reaction, then think on this: try telling the Inland Revenue you can't afford to pay your income tax. You see, the Inland Revenue is not stupid; they know damn well that if they let us get our hands on our pay, and out of that we have to pay them; we won't have the money left at the end of the month. So to make sure they get their share, they take it out of our pay packet **before** we get our mitts on it. So the very best way to ensure you save enough for your retirement is to do exactly the same thing.

This is no different from having pension contributions deducted from your pay in the UK. In fact if you choose to join the new Kiwisaver in New Zealand, it's exactly what is going to happen. The money you put into Kiwisaver is going to be taken out of your pay packet before you ever see it. If you have never done this yourself, it is daunting, but you **will** get used to it, and once you do it and see your savings growing month after month, it's incredibly motivating.

You need to bite the bullet, and sort out your budget to find the 10%. Most people take the 10% out of their take home pay, but some work it out based on their before-tax pay. If you just cannot make the numbers work for you at this stage, then make your savings as much as you can, and work up to 10% as you become used to it. The important thing to start with is to get used to putting the money aside as soon as you get paid, not saving what is left at the end of the month. The first time we worked like this, we were only saving 5%. We managed to stretch it to 10% of our take home pay, by being more ruthless with our budget, and using pay rises. We are looking at making it 10% of our before tax pay as soon as we can.

Where to find your 10%

- Budgeting: be ruthless.
- Pay rises, instead of using the extra money for spending – add it to your savings.
- Debts: Once you have paid off your debts – use the money you were paying as your savings – you are used to not spending it on stuff anyway!
- A second income: if two of you are earning, then use one of the incomes for investing for the future. Doing this also means that in the event of illness or redundancy, you are able to pare down and live on one income and you avoid "the two income trap".

There is no easy way out of this. We now need to be responsible for our own retirement, because there really is unlikely to be any state help for us. And besides: who wants to wait till they are 65 to retire anyway?

SO I'VE SAVED THE MONEY, HOW DO I KNOW WHAT TO INVEST IN?

> *"An investment in knowledge always pays the best interest"*
> Benjamin Franklin

You learn.

If you think that is difficult, bear this in mind: it's a whole lot **more** difficult to learn how to walk. You did that when you were a baby! Learning about investing isn't half as difficult as people want you to think it is. Hell, I've learned – and I was a financial Muppet!

Something I found amazing once I got to New Zealand was the number of free investment seminars available. These cover all sorts of investments and money making methods, from property, to shares, to currency exchange and a few things I can't even spell! I think a lot of these seminars are actually a good way to learn something about investing.

You should always be aware that often a free seminar will spend about a third of the time selling you a course –which will probably be fairly expensive. Not that it's always a bad course but you should "never sign anything" without sleeping on it first! Often they will want you to sign up immediately – but I really disagree with that approach. Some seminars you need to pay for (often less than $50 but be cheeky and ask for a free ticket!) Still be wary. If you are the sort of person who easily gets signed up for stuff, don't go. Or at least don't take your credit card or you may end up with that much-hated timeshare in Lanzarote! (Which is not a whole lotta use once you are all the way down here).

Personally I have learned a huge amount from the free seminars I have been to, and while I have signed up for some further courses, I have always taken my time to think it over fully first. (Ooh; have to admit though; there was one seminar I went to for a course, and the presenter mentioned that the 2-day course (at a cost of just under $1,000) involved walking on fire. 😊 I signed up for that immediately – call me crazy – but we do after all live in New Zealand – adventure capital of the world!)

If you are just starting out and want some basic information – check out the papers for free seminars. If you like the sound of any further courses, it's well worth doing a Google search on the company involved. You may find some interesting stuff. You can almost guarantee not all of it will be good, but it's up to you to decide what you believe, and what fits in with your plans.

In a nutshell, you can go one of two ways when you want to invest:

- Do it yourself, and invest directly which includes;
    - Bank accounts and term deposits (held for a specified period of time)
    - Property Investments
    - Buying shares

- Get someone else to do it for you;
    - Managed funds or unit trusts
    - Pension schemes
    - Kiwisaver

Which you choose depends really on how involved you want to be with your investments. Most people tend to get someone else to do the investing for them. This is exactly what I used to do in the UK, when I knew absolutely nowt about money. Now I've taken control of the investing, and work out what I want to do myself. It's more work certainly, but I get a lot of pleasure out of it.

If you invest yourself, you buy whatever shares, or property you like the look of, or find a bank account that pays you enough interest to suit your needs. Whereas with a managed fund, pension or unit trust, you would put your savings each month into a fund, and then the fund manager takes all the other savings that everyone else paid in that month, and he picks a load of shares to buy with all that money (having taken some of the money out for fees of course). I read somewhere recently that if you throw darts at a list of shares you would probably pick just as well as the fund managers do. Apparently – if you get a monkey to throw darts at a list of shares – they pick better performing shares. Life truly is bizarre sometimes.

PENSIONS, SHARES OR PROPERTY?

"Would you tell me which way I ought to go from here?"
asked Alice.
"That depends a good deal on where you want to get,"
said the Cat.
"I really don't care where," replied Alice.
"Then it doesn't much matter which way you go," said the Cat.
Lewis Carroll,
Alice's Adventures in Wonderland

Company pensions are available in New Zealand but most companies will not pay contributions into them because they have to pay Fringe Benefit Tax to the government in order to do so. So for every $100 they pay into your pension, they have to pay 33% in tax on top. Also, any contributions **you** personally pay into your pension scheme are made after you have paid income tax on the money earned. So you do not even get a tax benefit. Most New Zealand pensions invest heavily in New Zealand or Australian funds, so they tend to not do as well as they could if they invested worldwide.

Recently – there has been a new scheme released – called Kiwisaver, which is a private pension scheme, and is pretty much set to take over from any other pension schemes. I'll cover that separately as it really does need a chapter all to itself.

One of the problems with getting someone else to run your investments, quite apart from you not having personal control over them, is that many managed funds buy shares purely on the basis of how popular the shares are, not on whether they are good value or not. The problem with this is that the more popular a share is, the more it costs.

Now this popularity is pretty important to understand in any investing you are going to do, whether it's shares, property or pensions/managed funds. Oddly, when people buy investments, it's exactly what tends to happen, so let's look at it step by step. If you can get your head round this – you are way in front of most people when it comes to understanding investing, and it's actually quite simple:

- When an investment is popular, the price goes up because everyone wants to buy it.
- When an investment is not popular, the price goes down because no one wants to buy it.
- Most people buy an investment when the price is high, because it's popular.
- Most people sell an investment when the price is low, because the price is dropping and they are scared to lose money.
- You only actually lose money if you sell shares for less than you bought them.

Got it?

Now ask yourself these questions:
- Why would you a pay a high price to buy an investment, and sell it when the price goes down?
- Why not buy when everyone else is selling and the price is low, hang onto it, and sell it when it becomes popular and the price is high?

Aha, I know what you're thinking:

- How do I know the price won't go down further?
- Should I wait till the price drops more before I buy?
- Should I wait till the price goes up some more before I sell?
- How do I know what price I should pay for the investment in the first place?

Well, the best way to find that out is to get yourself educated about buying shares and other investments and then get some advice. Who to go to for that advice is the tricky bit. I have no easy answers for you, I'm afraid. I would say, however that it pays to really look around; don't go with the first Financial Advisor you come across. This is where it is really well worth learning about investing before you go to see an advisor, because you need to know whether they are talking sense, or talking rubbish. You need to be able to ask questions: why are they recommending these shares, or that investment; what are the risks; the pros and cons; would they let their mother invest in it; and most importantly: do they invest in them it themselves! I think you really need to know if your investment advisor is actually making money investing in the things he is telling you to spend your money on! Many of them don't. Many advisors make money by **selling** investments, not by investing. I personally think it's vitally important to understand this difference, and get advice off the people who actually invest.

We came across a company based in Christchurch called Wise Planning. They ran one of those free seminars, and I learned a huge amount just from that. One of the things we really liked about Wise Planning is that the boss is an active investor: he actually does what he was teaching us to do. We became clients of theirs, and started learning how to buy shares: what to look for, and how to work out what to pay. They use a technique called Value Investing. Basically you look for a company that is financially sound, but whose shares are not popular, so the price is below what it really should be. Then you buy shares in that company and wait for it to become popular. Remember, most people buy shares when the company is popular, and end up paying more than they should, so that's potentially a great time for the educated investor to sell.

If you can't get your head round that: pretend you are going to buy a new washing machine. You have spotted the latest whizzbang model. Would you really go into a store and ask to pay $200 more than the washing machine's retail price because it's the next best thing? Of course not: in fact you are more likely to ask for some form of discount. So **why on earth** do people pay more for shares than they are worth?

For some reason we have got it into our heads that shares are some freaky complicated things, and our brains dribble out of our ears. But really it's a simple principle: buy shares when they are in the "sale", and sell when everyone else is running a popularity contest over them.

If you don't have the confidence or the desire to learn how to choose shares yourself (because let's face it, it just may not appeal to you), then managed funds of some sort are probably your best option. There's nothing wrong with this; it's a perfectly valid way of investing for your future. The thing to watch for here is the huge fee's you may be charged. Even though someone else is running the fund for you, you should still keep an eye on it to make sure it's bringing you the returns you want. If it isn't, don't be afraid to change tack, and move to another fund. This is your future you are looking at, and it pays never to be totally hands off about it.

Now, the final thing I think you need to get your head round with shares or managed funds is **not to panic when the share market crashes**. Just like buying shares above, this is actually a great thing when you are buying your investment. All of a sudden, pretty much **every share is on sale** ☺. For the same amount of savings each month, you can suddenly get a lot more shares to add to your retirement fund. And yet what do most of us do? We panic that our investment is worth nothing, **and sell it!** ☹ Which is exactly the time when serious investors take advantage and start buying! Let's get one thing clear: a share market crash is a problem if you **need** to sell your investment. If you are still buying: get real happy, 'cos it's like the Boxing Day sales for shares.

Honestly – I believe that this is the one thing we need to get our heads round about investing. I was gobsmacked when I was first taught this (within 3 months of arriving in New Zealand). I'm pretty educated, don't consider myself exactly stupid; and yet it never occurred to me not to panic when share prices drop. No one had ever told me in simple terms how this works. And to be perfectly frank I'm more than a bit peeved by that.

If you want to do your own thing, and I've met a lot of Kiwis who do, then you **must** get educated. This is your retirement we are talking about, and it is daft to buy investments that you don't understand. **All investments carry risks**; you need to understand that and invest in something where you are comfortable with the level of risk involved. You will never be able to take the risk out completely, so don't even try.

> ### First Ranking Debenture Stocks - a cautionary tale.
>
> Do you have the foggiest idea what that means? No? Neither did thousands of Kiwis who invested over a billion dollars in them because they were offering returns (think interest) higher than the banks were offering on savings accounts. Some people put their life savings into them.
>
> What they did not understand was that First Ranking Debenture Stocks, are Mortgages. A bit like "Sub Prime" mortgages that we heard so much about in late 2007 and early 2008. Some of them are even worse, in that you are investing in car loans! Multiple investment companies, who were offering these investments to people, went bust during 2006 & 2007 in New Zealand. Wiping out those people's retirement funds with them. In February 2008, the 15th Finance company called in the liquidators.
>
> They owed 1700 investors $38.5 million (an average of $22,647 each). They had loaned out $41.8million to 32 borrowers in mortgages (an average of $1.3million each). Only one of those mortgages was behind in payments, and that was valued at $4.3million. That was enough to tip the balance and put the finance company into trouble.
>
> Most of the investors hadn't got the faintest idea they were investing in Mortgages or car loans (and worse, loans that were given to people who couldn't get lending from the main banks, so were always at a higher risk of defaulting, and default they did!).
>
> So I have a rule: If I don't know what it means, I don't invest in it. If I really want to invest in it anyway – I go and find out what it means. If I do know what it means, I find out how risky it is. Then I can decide whether it's for me or not. Never invest in something till you know what it is, and what the risks are.

A lot of Kiwis do go it alone with investment planning but invest in residential property. Property is big here; shares not so much as people got badly burned in the 1987 share market crash and won't look again. (i.e. they sold their shares when the market crashed, instead of buying shares in the sale.) Besides there are nice tax advantages (at the moment) to buying property and holding on to it while renting it out. If you want to buy property and "do it up" a la Property Ladder you will get taxed on the profit you make, but if you "buy and hold" you don't get taxed if it goes up in value.

Now, this is something that is vitally important to get right about investing in property in New Zealand. If you **intend** to sell a property at some point in the future for a profit; you should pay tax on the profit. There is no such thing as an amount of time you can safely hold it for and get away with selling at a profit without paying tax. Many people think that; but just because most people think it, it doesn't mean it is true. If you want to get into property, make absolutely sure you do it right, and document your intentions clearly at the outset. The only way not to have to pay tax on an investment property is never to sell it. Although the Inland Revenue **tends** not to charge tax on properties you have held for over 10 years, there is absolutely no rule that says that is the case. If you buy a property and intend to sell it after 10 years, you should pay tax on the profit.

Many people who do invest in property are about to come a cropper here in New Zealand, because they have not been paying their taxes properly on houses they have sold for profit. The Inland Revenue has been given a war chest of over $14m to chase Property Investors for unpaid tax. If you are going to do it – do it right. Never annoy the taxman! According to a briefing to the incoming Minister of Revenue for 2005: it was estimated that New Zealanders owed the Inland Revenue $1.5

Billion in unpaid taxes. Unfortunately, they are going after property investors first to get some of that back.
www.ird.govt.nz/aboutir/reports/briefing/briefing-2005

If you want to get into investing in property, you **must still** get educated. This is vitally important because you can lose a lot of money if you do not know what you are doing. In New Zealand – I would suggest looking at two websites:
www.richmastery.com
and
www.propertytalk.co.nz

Richmastery are "Property Educators" and sell courses to teach you about Property Investing. They also sell investment properties. It's all a bit cheesy on their website to be honest, and if you go for one of their free seminars you **will** face a medium to hard sell depending on the presenter. If you look behind that though, the education can be really helpful. Richmastery are responsible for making more millionaires in New Zealand than any other company; so if you find that interesting, go to one of their "Profit From Property" Seminars (remembering to leave your credit card at home if in danger of signing up without thinking it over), and see what you think. This seminar intends to sell tickets to Richmastery's 3-day Property Academy: an incredibly intensive nuts-and-bolts course, which gives you all the basic information in a one-hit, sleep-deprived, sugar-rush-fueled weekend.

We actually became their clients and joined their year-long mentoring program, although we decided not to attend the academy. We have found it hugely helpful in getting us going and showing us the ropes (without the sleep deprivation and sugar overload). This makes for much fun on the Property Talk website, as many of the posters take a pretty dim view of those of us who: (a) are too stupid to work it out for ourselves, and (b) pay Richmastery to teach us what to do.

Well, 😏 I say to that!

For a start, investing in anything was new to us, let alone property. Added to that, we were also new to New Zealand, and things are just different here. There's a lot to learn if you go down this route, and we felt it was well worth the money to get someone to help us do it right. Beside, why waste time, effort and in some cases money, when I can get someone who has already done it, to teach me faster and help me along the way, and stop me from making (expensive) mistakes.

Property Talk is a forum with a mix of old-time and new investors. It's worth noting that Property Talk members generally have an awful lot to say about Richmastery. It's usually very colourful 😊 (in fact their most popular thread is about the evils (some real – some imagined) of that company and if you think immigration forums can get a bit ripe sometimes: you aint seen nothing yet!) Also, while there is a lot of information on Property Talk: much of it like this book, is opinion, and should be taken as such. I also find the site quite intimidating and some of the posters on there can be utterly obnoxious, especially to new people who are just learning the ropes. For all that you can learn quite a bit, just remember you need a thick skin, and should you decide to try Richmastery, it's best not to mention that on Property Talk.

Do be aware that most people "negative gear" property these days, which means they make a loss week to week. (The rent does not cover the mortgage and costs of the property). This is because at the moment, house prices and interest rates are high, and rents have not caught up with that. The Government pays you some of that money back if you are a taxpayer, if you have your business set up correctly (see chapter on LAQ Whats?). You **do need to have spare cash to "prop up" a property if you are going to do this**, and it does limit how many properties you can buy.

In the past it's been possible to buy what are called "Positive Cashflow Properties" which means that the rent more than covers the mortgage on a property, plus any fees, and you get money left over! Nice, but not easy to find at this time with house prices and interest rates going up much faster than rents. Property moves in cycles; so at some point the rents should go up and the interest rates go down, but for the moment, you will probably need cash to hold onto a rental property in most areas of New Zealand.

Now, just to clear something up, which I will cover in more depth in a later chapter: If your investment property makes a loss, then **you do not get the whole of that loss back from the government**. You only get some of it back. **You** have to fund the rest of the shortfall.

CAN'T I JUST PUT MY MONEY IN THE BANK AND LET IT GROW?

*You are worth what you saved,
not the millions you made.*
John Boyle O'Reilly

What if you decide you really do not want to learn about investing? What about putting your money in the bank and earning interest? Well, it's great to have some money in the banks, but remember, there are still risks involved in that too. If you really thought banks were a risk free place to put your money, try talking to anyone who had money in Northern Rock! It has happened here in New Zealand as well; apparently BNZ (Bank of New Zealand – of the credit card debacle) has been bailed out twice in its history by the New Zealand government, which is hardly surprising given the way they treat their customers (and staff).

The biggest thing you need to be aware of with money in the banks is that although you may get a healthy interest rate (about 7-8% in 2007), you pay tax on that. You also have to take into account inflation.

Now inflation was also another of those things that baffled me; but like many things, I'm convinced the powers-that-be simply have a vested interest in making it sound more complicated than it really is. Inflation is just a smart-arsed way of saying that a penny sweet now costs 10p. So while 10p used to buy you 10 sweets, now it only buys you one. In another 20 years time, you will probably need a pound to buy a "penny sweet".

So the money you leave in the bank, even though it earns interest, won't be "worth" as much in the future as it is now.

Depressingly, it is now estimated that to have a "millionaire lifestyle" you need to have $25 million in the bank – that's inflation for you.😲

So, let's assume you have $10,000 in the bank and you leave it there gathering interest for 10 years. What effect would a tax rate of 20% make? Well, that takes the interest rate to an effective 5.6%. Already it's not looking too good. Now let's account for inflation, which is about 3%. You have to now take that away from your post-tax interest rate (because while your money is growing at 5.6%, the cost of living is growing at 3%, so the actual buying power of your money is only growing by 2.6%).

Fund in Bank For 10 years @ 7%	Interest only	Interest – Tax	Interest – tax and inflation
10,000	20,136	17,506	13,498

One thing you really need to understand about money in the bank is that after the 10 years (assuming you pay 20% tax) you will **actually** have $17,506 sitting in there, but it will **only be worth** the equivalent of $13,498 in today's money. It's not great news is it?

Now, something that I know quite a few people think of doing, is investing money in Premium Bonds. So I think it's worth just saying a few things about that. One of the things that people like about this is that the "capital" is guaranteed. That means that if you put £10,000 into Premium Bonds, no matter what happens, you cannot lose your £10,000. No matter how good property or shares are as an investment, there is never a guarantee that you will not lose your money. However: remember that annoying "inflation" stuff? £10,000 won't buy you anywhere near as many penny sweets in 10 years time as it did when you put the money into premium bonds. So while yes, you will still have £10,000, it won't be worth as much. Also, with the best will in the world, Premium Bonds are a **gamble** not an investment. You may make some money on it, but if you do, it is entirely based on chance. If your numbers come up, you win some money. If your numbers do not come up, you don't make any money. When you invest; the aim is to make money while you sit on the beach sipping a cold drink, not to have to hope that a Random Number Generator spits out the right number for you.

If you want to see what chance you have of actually winning anything on the Premium Bonds: pop along to Moneysavingexpert.com. They now have this really cool toy where you can put in the amount you are thinking of "investing" in premium bonds: and it will tell you how much money you are unlikely to make on it. If you still want to put money in Premium Bonds: that's fine; just do it with open eyes and knowing that there is a risk of not making any money on it, and that your capital is going to go down in value.

So, which is better? Shares; managed funds; property; or the bank.

Or after that lot of utterly depressing news do you feel like stuffing it under the mattress anyway? Well, that's one of those things I just can't answer, I'm sorry. It's up to each of us to really look at our personal situation, our preferences, and our ability to tolerate risk. It's also up to us to learn which we prefer. We started out with shares, but decided in the end that property was more suitable for us. That may not be the case for you and your family. Think about what **you** want out of **your** retirement, and how much effort you want to put into running **your** investments **yourself**.

Remember: the main thing that makes investing risky is ignorance. If you don't understand what you are doing and the exact risks involved, you shouldn't do it. There has to be an amount of personal responsibility taken for your future so if this is still all gobbledygook, then read some books and understand it. A really good start would be Robert Kiyosaki's Rich Dad Poor Dad (there's actually a series of them but the first one is a classic). It's very easy to read and to understand – no economics degree required. In fact, it was this book that made me decide to change from concentrating solely on investing in shares, to including property. I would also recommend a Kiwi book called "Pension Panic" by Gareth Morgan. This is a very frank look at the state of the future of Kiwi retirement. Worth reading if you honestly think that you can manage on the state pension.

We have now stopped buying shares completely, other than continuing to pay into our UK Endowment fund (which is a type of managed fund), and are concentrating on buying property. This is because we find property easier to understand (I get mortgages and interest rates a lot more than I get financial statements of businesses, which send me to sleep), but also because we enjoy it more. We are having huge amounts of fun with it, and while at the moment it's quite scary: all we are hearing is that the housing market is crashing, just like with shares; that should mean that houses can be bought at "sale prices".

Whatever you decide; you need to do something. Do not rely on a state pension. It makes for a fairly depressing retirement.

Costs of our Education

Over the past 3 years we have paid out quite a sum of money for our education in investing. So I thought it would be a good idea to actually show you exactly what we paid, and why we decided to change.

Wise Planning

The initial seminar was free. That ran for 3-4 hours and was packed with information, a lot of which was incredibly helpful in its own right. We then decided to join their coaching course, called The Money Matrix. The fee for the first year was $5,181, and that was going to be followed each year for the next two years with fees of $1,500 per year. Now that sounds like a whole lotta cash, but to be honest what we learned in that first year was worth a whole lot more to us. In fact we worked out that using information in that course, would over time, make us hundreds of thousands of dollars. (That's in saved interest, better money management, better budgeting, and investing.)

Where we hit a problem was that, with no notice, the fee for the 2nd and 3rd years doubled. I was incredibly peeved, because apart from anything, we had budgeted for the fee for the past year, and having to find almost double the amount really screwed up my budget. I felt this was utterly wrong and we complained to the boss. He was not particularly pleasant about it to be honest. ("Wealthy" people would see this as an "opportunity" 😊) We decided to pay the second year fee, and see if we got our moneys worth (we were told that our "extra investment" would be matched with extra "value" – it wasn't, and the communication was just as bad the second year). So we left the scheme after the second year.

Richmastery.

We didn't pay for the Profit From Property Seminar. That was another 3 hours, and again actually gave us quite a lot of useful information in its own right. However, we decided the Academy wasn't for us. Instead we took the longer-term approach, and chose the Mentoring. That cost $6,000 for a year. (The academy would have cost about the same amount).

Something that really made us realise that there was a difference in value is that with the Wise Planning system: we met our "coach" 4 times in 2 years, and only once got to mix with other people on the course (and we had to pay an extra $500 for that). Whereas with the Mentoring: we got 11 monthly meetings with a group of other students, and we also got 6 one-on-one sessions with the coach. We decided it just wasn't worth another year at Wise Planning. We also increased our personal wealth a lot faster in the year with Richmastery than we did in 2 years with Wise Planning.

Books.

In addition to the courses, we have also spent a couple of hundred dollars on books. A lot of books we have simply borrowed from the library, but as we honestly do love reading and owning books, we also buy the better ones to keep. You can learn an awful lot from books alone, and it is a lot cheaper than attending seminars and courses. However, for us, we actually found the seminars were where we made the most progress.

WHAT IS KIWISAVER?

Kiwis wanting to get on top of money management need to apply their DIY attitude – not look to a financial Fairy Godmother to do it for them.
Gareth Morgan
www.gmk.co.nz

Kiwisaver is a new Pension scheme that started running on 1st July 2007. New Zealand needs more people to save more money (in fact – most countries do – including the UK). So the government finally set up Kiwisaver to try and encourage more people to save. It is **not** compulsory (**yet**).

So – what are the main things you need to know?

- Kiwisaver is a long-term savings plan that is backed (not guaranteed) by the New Zealand Government.
- When you start a new job – you will automatically be signed up for Kiwisaver
- If you do not want to be a part of it – you need to "Opt Out"
- You can save either 4% or 8% of your gross (pre-tax) salary into Kiwisaver.
- Your employer now has to give you a contribution as well – 1% for the next year (2008), then rising to 2% in 2009, and maxing out at 4% from 2011 onwards.
- The Inland Revenue takes the money from your salary through the PAYE system and gives it to the Kiwisaver fund you have chosen.

- If you do not choose your own fund – it goes into a "Default" fund – one of several that the government set up with various companies for just this event.
- The government gives you a $1,000 "Kick start" when you join as a sweetener.
- The government also gives you up to $20 a week as another incentive.
- The government also gives you $40 a year towards the fees of running your Kiwisaver fund.
- You can "divert" half your contributions towards paying off your mortgage after the first year.
- If you are a First Home Buyer – you can choose to access the funds in your Kiwisaver account after three years in order to buy your first home. You cannot take out the $1,000 Kickstart, or the government contribution of $20 a week, or the employer contributions – those must stay in the fund.
- If you are a First Home Buyer – the government **may** give you another $1,000 for every year you have been a contributing member (up to a maximum of $5,000) towards a deposit.

Now – the things you **really** need to know!

1/ The 4% or 8% is calculated on your before tax (gross) pay, but taken out of your after tax (net) pay
So it's actually **more** than 4% or 8% of your **take home** pay
For example – if we go back to the 2008 Inland Revenue PAYE / Kiwisaver calculator, and now ask it to look at our Kiwisaver deductions as well – we get:

CALCULATION	Monthly Pay	4% PRE TAX	4% AFTER TAX
Gross income (Salary / Wage)	$6,250.00	$6,250.00	$6,250.00
Kiwisaver Deductions (pre tax)	$0.00	$250.00	$0.00
PAYE Deductions (including ACC Levy)	$1,675.26	$1,573.73	$1,675.26
Kiwisaver Deductions (post tax)	$0.00	$0.00	$250.00
Student Loan Deductions	$0.00	$0.00	$0.00
Net Payment (i.e. What ends up in your pocket)	$4,574.74	$4,426.27	$4,324.74

So why is there a difference? Why do I care? Why am I peeved about it?

Well, in the Pre-Tax scenario – what happens is that you earn $6250 a month, $250 is diverted to Kiwisaver, and then you get taxed on what is left – ($6,000). So the $250 going into your Kiwisaver account is actually only costing you about $150 out of your take home pay. Which is quite snazzy really. This is the same as making a Private Pension Contribution in the UK.

However – what happens because it's all done after-tax is that they work out your 4% and say that you have to put $250 aside. They tax the whole of your income of $6250, and take out the tax. **Then** they swipe the $250. Which means that unlike the first case, in order to put $250 into Kiwisaver – you actually have to lose $250 out of your pocket each month. And incidentally – while in both cases you are contributing 4% of your **gross** salary – in the first case it works out at 3.3% of your **take home** pay, whereas after tax, it works out at a whopping **5.6% of your take home pay.**

You need to aware of this. **Do not** think of the Kiwisaver contribution as 4% of your take home pay – because it's not.

2/ You cannot access the fund till you are 65 years old.

The age at which you can take out your Kiwisaver fund is linked to the age at which you receive New Zealand state superannuation. At the moment, that is age 65, but may change in the future.

If you use the fund as a First Time Homebuyer, then you can access it early. In which case you can get the money plus up to $5,000 homebuyers bonus. You cannot take out the $1,000 kick-start or the $20 tax credits early. You cannot take out the employer's contributions early.

3/ The $5,000 first-home-buyers deposit subsidy is going to be run by Housing New Zealand.
Not everyone will be eligible for it.
According to the HNZC website:

How do I know whether I am eligible for the first home deposit subsidy?

First home deposit subsidies will become available from July 2010 to members who joined KiwiSaver in July 2007. They must have regularly contributed around 4% of their income for three years to become eligible to apply for the subsidy (ie, regularly contributing from 2007 to be eligible for the subsidy in 2010 at the earliest).

To be eligible for the first home deposit subsidy, you must:
- Be a member of a KiwiSaver scheme, or a complying superannuation fund

> - Have a household income (before tax) of less than $100,000 per year (for one or two people), or less than $140,000 per year (for more than two people)
> - Be purchasing a lower-quartile priced home. (As an example, currently this is $400,000 for higher priced areas such as North Shore City, Auckland City and Queenstown Lakes District, and $300,000 for the rest of New Zealand).
> - ***The eligibility criteria relating to the income caps and regional house price caps will be reviewed in 2009 before the policy takes effect.***

(I.e. – they can change their mind just before all those hardworking contributors get their hands on the money – but it could just be that I'm a bit cynical!)

4/ The $20 a week tax credit is only paid at the end of the year.

This means that you miss out on any interest or growth on the $20 a week through out the year. Admittedly, it's not a lot of money, but dammit, it's money you should get every week, not once a year!

5/ Just try getting a pay rise for the next few years.

Your boss automatically now has to fund an extra 1% per year on your salary. Now the thing is, your employer actually gets a tax break to cover this, but just be aware that they may try to reduce your pay rises as well.

Incidentally – the calculators you can use to see how much your contributions add up to over time are all assuming that you will get a 3.5% pay rise **every year** as well as the employer Kiwisaver contribution. The thing is that they then increase your contributions in line with that, and work out your possible pension pot on that basis.

Bear this in mind when you see those really big numbers!

6/ You need to think very carefully before assuming that Mortgage Diversion is worth it for you.

Remember, you can only move half of **your** contribution. You cannot move half of the employer contribution, or half of the tax credits. You also only get tax credits for the half of your contribution that you don't divert.

This means that in order to pay into the mortgage diversion and still get the maximum tax credits, you need to be able to pay $40 a week into Kiwisaver. That allows you to divert $20 a week into your mortgage and still be contributing $20 a week into Kiwisaver which gets you the $20 a week tax credit.

The thing is that you need an income of $52,000 a year to allow you to pay $40 a week into Kiwisaver as your 4% of gross salary.

If you earn less than that, your 4% does not give you a high enough contribution to allow you to divert half your payment into the mortgage without losing some of your tax credit.

More importantly in many ways: do you really need to divert the extra into your mortgage? Bear in mind that although it will help you pay off your mortgage earlier, it is also affecting the amount of money you have to retire on. You could be putting off building up a retirement nest egg, and if you don't have any other form of retirement savings – that is not a good idea.

I really suggest that if you are planning on looking at Kiwisaver and using the mortgage diversion – you get an advisor to work out the sums for you and look at whether it is really worth it for you. We certainly made the decision that while we go to great lengths to pay off the mortgage fast – we are also making plans to have a very nice retirement pot as well.

7/ The $20 a week tax credits are not paid to anyone under 18 years old.
Bear this in mind if you are thinking of opening up a Kiwisaver account for your children. It sounds like a great idea, but only the savings you put in the fund for them will grow. Do not rely on the Tax Credit – cos it ain't coming.

Children will however get the $1,000 Kickstart payment, which could be worth a nice packet over time. Do your sums carefully and see if that is enough of a sweetener to make up for the lack of the tax credit. There are fund providers available that allow you to open the fund, get the $1,000 and then not have to pay anything else into them. It's worth getting some advice on.

Also, if you sign your children up for a fund, the rules at the moment say that once they start a job, they will automatically start paying the 4% contribution and don't get to opt out, as they are not signing up from scratch. It's not really a bad thing as it will mean they straightaway get into the habit of saving - but you may have to explain why you did it to a disgruntled teenager.

8/ Under 18's who work are not eligible for employer contributions.
So while they can pay 4% or 8% of their pay into Kiwisaver, and get the $1,000 Kickstart, they may not get any other benefits till they are 18 years old. It is at the employer's

discretion, so your child may get contributions matched by their employer, or they may not.

9/ You need to keep an eye on the fees.

There can be up to 6 separate fees on each Kiwisaver fund. And those are just the ones they **have** to tell you about.

- Entry or Exit fees
- Switch fees (if you want to change funds)
- Fund Management fees (usually a % of the fund)
- Trustees fee (another % of the fund)
- An admin fee – usually a fixed amount per month.
- A Mortgage Diversion fee.

For more information on the fee situation, it's worth having a look at Gareth Morgan's website: www.gmk.co.nz. Gareth Morgan runs a Kiwisaver fund, but claims that he is running it very differently than most, including being upfront about the fee structure.

Bear in mind that the fees will be shown in any Investment statements you get before opening your fund. I know - no one reads these brochures, but it is something you need to do. Remember – this is your retirement fund. If you don't have any other retirement savings, isn't it worth actually looking at the brochure and reading it? If you don't understand what it says (because I never did), then ask someone.

10/ The Online calculators are a touch misleading.
All the calculators I've seen which show in nice big numbers what your fund is going to be worth state that they do not take into account the fees and rely on a 3.5% yearly pay rise! Bear this in mind!

11/ You need to look at the quoted returns offered.

Many of the quoted returns for the "Default" funds are way less than the banks are paying if you put your money in a normal savings account. And you still have to pay fees on top. Now it's fair to say that because Kiwisaver is so new; no one really knows how well the funds are going to do. In a few years, we will have some idea, but for now, and for quite a long time to come, we just are not able to have any real idea how well our money will do in Kiwisaver.

This alone isn't a reason not to join; but it is something you need to be aware of.

Most of the "Low Risk" funds invest only in Cash (i.e.- stick the money in a bank). So you end up getting bank interest rates, only with loads of fees taken out!

12/ Kiwisaver is not guaranteed by the New Zealand Government.

Like any other investment you may not get back all the money you put into it. The Tax Credits and Kickstart should offset that, but still, you need to be aware that there is no guarantee that Kiwisaver will in fact provide you with the money you are expecting it to.

There is also no guarantee that a future government will not do a "Gordon Brown UK Style Tax Grab" at some point and nick a huge chunk of your pension!

The "Government Backing" simply means that the New Zealand government thinks it's a great idea, and will give tax credits and a sweetener to start with to entice you to join the scheme.

13/ Your employer and the Inland Revenue do not pass on your contributions to your fund immediately.

In fact after several months of Kiwisaver being active, some people had still not had any of their contributions paid into their funds. In the long run, this really won't hurt too much when looking at the amount of money you should end up with; for me it's a principle thing. It's fair to say though, that I feel putting the Inland Revenue in charge of paying funds into peoples pensions is a really silly thing to do anyway.

In theory, the Inland Revenue can hang on to your contributions for up to 3 months before depositing them in your chosen fund.

14/ Watch your employment contracts carefully.

Some employers are now writing job contracts with the Kiwisaver contributions included in your total package. For example: if your employer is offering you a salary of $75,000 a year; your 4% comes out of that, but so does **their** 4%. The government has apparently closed the loophole that allows this – but just be careful. Bear in mind that your employer gets a tax break to cover your contribution – so they should not be doing this.

15/ You cannot opt out of Kiwisaver during the first 2 weeks in a new job.

This means that you need to take into account that you will likely lose 5.6% of your take home pay from your first pay packet or two (or more) whether you like it or not.

Your employer cannot stop the deductions until they get notification from the IRD to do so. At that point, if your employer hasn't passed on the money to the IRD, you can get it straight back. Otherwise you have to wait till the IRD gives it back (they will pay you interest on it though – which is nice of them I guess).

Your employer is obligated to tell you that you can opt out of Kiwisaver, and they have to give you the form that allows you to do so. I have however heard of employers that do not do this.

Now – something I really want to get you to understand about this: I've heard many people saying that they will join Kiwisaver for the "Free Money" that the government is going to give them – that is the $1,000 kick start and the $20 a week tax credit. Well, maybe it's just my innate distrust of the government – but it's not really free money: it's money they took off you in taxes and are now (thoughtfully) giving you back, as long as you don't want to spend it till you are 65. It was your money in the first place. I guess it's down to your view on taxes as to whether that will annoy the hell out of you or not. Maybe it's worth joining just to get your tax back?

Please get some advise on Kiwisaver before just blindly opening an account and hoping for the best. In writing this chapter, I found it very hard to get clear information. Thanks goes to Alan Borthwick at FSB4 Financial in Wellington for helping me get my head round the most complicated bits. Kiwisaver could be a very nice plan for those people who do not want to do it the way we do, and sort out their own financial future. You do need to do something about your retirement, so if you think Kiwisaver is for you, then speak to a financial planner and get some plans drawn up.

For us: it would only be worth it if we could find a company that would allow us to put in a minimum payment of $20 a week. So my husband can't do a scheme through work where he has to divert at least 4%. If you could put in the $20, you get the $1,000 kickstart, plus the government adds its $20 a week. Each year: you double your money, and that's before you take into account the $1,000! And remember you can set up Kiwisaver accounts for children, for whom over time it can create a very nice pot, even without the $20 a week tax credit.

The thing to bear in mind is that Kiwisaver, like any managed fund or pension is a long-term investment. It's not something you are going to "get rich quick" with by any means, but over time you could potentially get a nice little nest egg. Because it's so long-term, you are able to ride out the peaks and troughs of the share market, housing market or any other market your fund invests in. When the markets are crashing, your contributions are buying more investments, and when the market is doing well, your contributions do not buy as much, but the fund you have so far is growing well.

As with any investment, your main problem is what happens when you come to retirement age, and you want the money. Generally speaking, you would need to keep an eye on your Kiwisaver fund, and as you get nearer to retirement age, you would look to change funds into a less risky one; at that point maybe go for a cash fund and keep the money safe, even if it won't grow much more.

So all in all I'm personally not that impressed with Kiwisaver I have to say. I really believe that with the willingness to get a financial education you can beat the return on Kiwisaver quite nicely. And you are then also not subject to the whim of the government. If Gordon Brown could swipe £5 Billion out of our UK Pensions by introducing a new tax, then I'm a bit loath to trust the New Zealand government not to do the same.

I spoke to a few Financial advisors about this, and they are all for Kiwisaver, given that the Employers now have to match your contributions up to the 4% limit. And they do have a good point (much as I hate to admit it 😊). If you really are bad at saving, and have nothing behind you for retirement, and you really don't want to DIY with your future earnings, then grabbing an extra 4% to go into your pot – *which does not come out of your take home pay* – can be a real bonus (much more than the "cash back" the government is giving you).

However – they also all said that one of the things they really liked was that because it was a Government backed scheme, your money would be safe. They all went a bit white when I told them what the UK Government had done to people's pension pots. No one here seems to think the government would ever **dream** of doing such a thing. Apparently the news hasn't filtered down to the New Zealand financial services industry.

So I guess it comes down to: do you feel you can go it alone or do you feel you need a basic fund behind you as some security. If you are thinking about Kiwisaver – **please** – do lots of research and get lots of advice. It's fairly new and many advisors don't know much more about it than the man in the street – so make sure you question everything. And bear in mind that Kiwisaver is still an **investment -** there is risk involved. **You may not get back all the money you put into it - the same with any investment**. It's a rule that should never be forgotten. Time heals most wounds with investments, so even if there is a stock market crash, you should recover eventually – but it can hurt if you need to take the money when the crash happens!

Keep an eye on the Sorted Website (www.sorted.org.nz). This is run by the Retirement Commission and is probably the best resource for Kiwisaver. Best of all – I notice that they are adding to their calculators and information as more useful stuff comes from the fund providers. They still make assumptions about the funds that I think are misleading, but it is by far the best website I have yet seen for looking at Kiwisaver options.

I'm really sorry that I cannot be more upbeat about this. But the bottom line is – if you have no other retirement fund – and you don't have the knowledge to go it alone – then you really do have to consider opening a Kiwisaver account. I feel that even if you want to do some clever investing, such as buying Direct Shares, or Property, it doesn't hurt to have some sort of general fund behind you as well. We have an Endowment policy in the UK – which we don't actually need to pay off our mortgage, plus hubby's company pension with 10 years of contributions. For us, these act as a nice little backup, while we do our own thing.

If you wish to read a much more positive review of Kiwisaver, then look for a book by Mary Holm called "Kiwisaver" I disagree with almost everything she has to say about the scheme, so if you want to balance my admittedly "underwhelmed" point of view, then it's worth a read.

Mary says:
"Kiwisaver is so attractive that, arguably, all of us should sign ourselves up and perhaps our kids – even if we have to add to the mortgage to do it".

I have a real problem with telling people on low incomes (any income for that matter) to increase their debt to finance a product like Kiwisaver. Taking on **any** extra debt in order to invest increases your risk dramatically, and should **only** be done if you have got a damn good education in the subject and are fully aware of the risks involved and are prepared to take that risk.

If the investment does not perform the way people wish it to, and you take out a loan to pay for it, you can not only end up with less money than you paid in, but you can end up with not enough money to pay off the debt! Mary believes that the $1,000 Kickstart and the $20 tax credit wipe out any small issues such as bad returns, or increased debt repayments. I disagree. Totally.

So if you want to hear the other side, you really can't get more of an opposite point of view to mine than to read Mary Holm's book. It is also worth noting that it seems that this is the book that ASB Bank staff have been given in order to teach them the basics of Kiwisaver.

LAQ WHATS?

"I hold in my hand 1,379 pages of tax simplification."
Delbert L Latta

LAQC stands for Loss Attributing Qualifying Company. Clear as mud?

In English: it means that if you run a business, which is registered as an LAQC, you can offset any losses that company makes, against tax that you pay on a salary in another job. For example:

- You earn $75,000 a year in your job.
- You own an LAQC that makes a loss of $10,000 a year
- You only pay tax on an income of $65,000 a year.

I'll use Property, as it's what everyone talks about in terms of LAQC's here – but it does apply to **any** business. You buy a rental property in the name of an LAQC. The rent covers a proportion of the mortgage interest, but you still have rates to pay, property management fees, maintenance, insurance and a whole host of incidental expenses you wish you didn't have to pay for!

So – for example:
You buy a house for $250,000, and it rents out at $250 per week (rents in New Zealand are quoted per week, not per month). Your interest on that mortgage (say it's at 10%), is going to be $25,000 per year, and the rent will give you only $13,000 a year. 😢

Already you are quite a way out of pocket. Now add in a few thousand for expenses and fixed costs, say $5,000 a year.

Rent	13,000
Mortgage interest:	-25,000
Expenses	- 5,000
Loss =	-17,000

Now – something funny happens – you can "Depreciate" the building and just about everything in it – which adds to the loss. This is where things get cunning! You see – you can "make a loss on paper" that doesn't actually come out of your pocket – but gets added on to that $17,000 loss. Say for example, you manage to claim $17,000 yearly depreciation.

Rent	13,000
Mortgage interest:	-25,000
Expenses	- 5,000
Depreciation	-17,000
Loss =	-34,000

Now – you have "made a loss" of $34,000. The thing to get clear about here is that half that "loss" is only on paper. It's a figment of an accountant's imagination. You **only really** made a loss of $17,000.

So – you tell the Inland Revenue. And what they do – is take the whole $34,000 **off** your normal taxable income! So if you earn $75,000 a year, on which you would pay tax at a rate of 39% at the highest rate, they now say that you in fact only earned $41,000 a year, and you now only pay tax on that! Which is a bit cool.

So now, if we were to put that $41,000 salary into the same PAYE calculator that we used to work out your take home pay for your dream job offer; what does it tell us?

Well, according to the calculator, the monthly tax if you only earned $41,000 works out at $675.43. Whereas if the tax was worked out on the whole $75,000, it would be $1,675.26. That means that because you are running a business alongside earning your normal salary, you now pay over $1,000 less in tax each month out of that salary. The really cool thing is that some of that tax deduction comes from the "paper only" losses, not from money you actually lost.

CALCULATION	Normal	With LAQC
Gross income (Salary / Wage)	$6,250.00	$6,250.00
Kiwisaver Deductions	$0.00	$0.00
Paye Deductions (including ACC Levy) (2008 rates)	$1,675.26	$675.43
Net Payment (I.e. What ends up in your pocket)	$4,574.74	$5,574.57

So sorting everything out in the wash:

- You lost $17,000 in real money.
- You lost $17,000 in "figment of the imagination" money.
- The IRD gives you back about $12,000 over the year.
- So all in all, you had to put in only $5,000 of your own money.
- The government gives you $1,040 a year in "free" money for Kiwisaver, and here they give you $12,000.
- Weyhey!

In fact – where this gets **really** cool – is when you have a situation where you start making a bit of money – because you still get to claim your expenses and depreciation. If you look at exactly the same example as before – but now rents go up and start to cover the mortgage interest – you still get to claim a tax loss.

```
Rent                    25,000
Mortgage interest:     -25,000
Expenses                -5,000
Depreciation           -17,000
Loss                   -22,000
```

CALCULATION	Normal	With LAQC
Gross income (Salary / Wage)	$6,250.00	$6,250.00
Kiwisaver Deductions	$0.00	$0.00
Paye Deductions (including ACC Levy) (2008 rates)	$1,675.26	$1,019.80
Net Payment (I.e. What ends up in your pocket)	**$4,574.74**	**$5,230.20**

Now, I know that looks horrendously complicated and a bit of a maths nightmare, but if you can, bear with it a minute longer.

- You lost $5,000 in real money.
- You lost $17,000 in "figment of the imagination" money.
- The IRD gives you back about $8,400 over the year (in "free" money).
- So all in all, you make an extra $3,400.
- Weyhey!

Now – a warning – because some people do forget a very important fact about LAQC's and this reduction in tax. The government will **never** pay you all the money you "lose" in a business. You only ever get back the "Taxable Equivalent" of your loss. So if your tax rate is 19.5%, then you get 19.5% of the loss back. You still actually "lost" 80.5% of the money. If you rate in the 39% tax bracket – you still bear 61% of the loss. Your "paper losses" such as depreciation may not be enough to turn into profit.

So – what's the point you may ask? Well, there are a few things to consider:

1) Is the value of your business increasing enough that the loss in your pocket is outweighed by the increase in value? So – in property for example – is the value of the house rising faster than the amount you are topping it up by?

2) What can you claim as expenses – and does that make it worth it?
If you set up a "Cottage Industry" from home, or in fact ever use part of your home as an "Office" for the purpose of making some extra money – then you can use the running costs of that office as expenses. Suddenly – you can claim a proportion of your home mortgage interest, rates, electricity bills etc. as a business expense.

3) Does the depreciation in fact mean you end up with more money in your pocket each month than you had before? Sometimes it does.

4) With an LAQC, you can assign the losses to the shareholders for maximum benefit. So if there are two of you, and you are both shareholders; one of whom pays 39% tax and the other only pays 19.5%, then you can assign 99% of the shares to the higher tax payer, so 99% of the loss is offset against their tax. Only 1% is offset against the 19.5% tax. This maximizes the tax benefit.

5) If your Tax Rates change, then you can simply change the shareholding to carry on getting the most benefit.

You don't always have to have an LAQC to take advantage of these things; the LAQC is just a handy way of doing it. Always ensure that before embarking on anything like this that you get the advice of a very good accountant and probably a lawyer as well. The Inland Revenue does not take kindly to people who take the mick – so if you are planning on taking advantage of the tax rules in New Zealand – make real sure you do it properly from the outset. New Zealand is not so cute and cuddly a place that they take kindly to tax evasion. Saying "I didn't know" is not an effective defense with the taxman. Do it right and do it legally.

> You cannot use an LAQC solely for the purposes of paying less tax. You must intend that, at some point in the future, your company makes a profit and will start paying tax. The LAQC system is there to help get businesses up and running.

It's also worth noting that at the time of writing, with house prices hitting painfully high levels for most people: many people want to stop LAQC's being used by Property Investors. Personally, I think that's only fair if it applies to **everyone** who takes advantage of LAQC's, not just people who run property businesses. But it's worth bearing in mind and keeping an eye on. You **can** use an LAQC to run any type of business. It's also true that you can claim tax loses and use them against income from a salary without having an LAQC – the LAQC is just an easier way of doing it.

HEADS OR TAILS – THE NEW ZEALAND ECONOMY FOR NUMPTIES!

If all the economists were laid end to end,
they'd never reach a conclusion.
George Bernard Shaw

If the nation's economists were laid end to end,
they would point in all directions.
Arthur H. Motley

So, all in all – is the economy in New Zealand booming, busting, or living it up at the beach – and what has that got do with us anyway? Well, over the past few years, I've read a whole load of articles and opinion pieces about this subject, most of which were so utterly boring that it defies belief. And do you know what I've discovered? That basically, all these "experts" haven't really got a clue either!

I'm really not kidding. It doesn't matter whether they are going on about the economy, inflation, interest rates, the value of the dollar, or house prices. When you strip out all the emotional twaddle designed to get you in a panic and make a dull subject exciting – the majority of these articles can be summed up by:

- The Market could go up.
- The Market could go down.
- The Market could stay the same.

How utterly not-helpful was that????
Try it and see what you find. In the same article you will often find contradictory facts and figures. Often these are backed up

by quoting what was said in a similarly contradictory article of a few days earlier.

So if you, like me, feel that there's not a snowballs chance in hell of ever understanding economics – just bear this in mind – the economists talk a load of guff half the time anyway! And also remember:

> For every Economist –
> there is an equal and opposite Economist.

So if one writes something you don't like – find another article that does tell you what you want to hear! You will often find it on the next page of the same newspaper.

So, taking all that into account: what does it mean for us as migrants? Is the cost of living going up or down, and are our wages changing to cover that? Well, I've read many times over the past year or so that wages are going up – but hey just cos it's in a newspaper doesn't mean it's true. My understanding is that salaries are far from keeping up with the actual cost of living, rather than government "inflation", which seems to ignore a lot of the price increases. In that case, interest rates, local house prices and fuel / transport costs have all gone up hugely in the last year or so and wages have certainly not matched it. Interest rates are pegged to go up again (trying to stop the housing boom and to stop people going on spending binges).

The governor of The Reserve Bank Of New Zealand is intent on stopping inflation going up. He wants people to stop spending, because that will bring prices down. Apparently. It seems to be lost on him (and most economists) that putting up interest rates increases the cost of housing. But as that doesn't seem to get included in "Inflation figures" we are supposed to ignore it!

Also, most Kiwis have financial habits that are just as bad as us Brits. Household debt is spiraling here as much, if not more than, in the UK. This seems to have been fuelled by the increase in house values, and people spending equity as well as an increase in the "buy now pay later" mentality and constantly spending more money than is earned. It's matched with a lack of saving – which is in part why the Government has introduced Kiwisaver. The vast majority of any investing is done in the housing market only; mainly because it's easier to understand for a lot of people than stocks and shares, and you get the really great tax benefits.

My feeling is that if you are pretty wised up financially and know how to handle money (spending less than you earn and making some plans for your future finances) then you can do pretty well here. But if you aren't – it can hurt a lot.

I would also caution anyone who feels that coming to live in New Zealand will automatically change your spending habits. New Zealanders are just as likely to spend on credit as anyone else in the western world. Apparently as of 2007; the average Kiwi spends $1.15 for every $1 they earn. So if you want to cut out on consumerism – then you have to do it the hard way and make the choice not to spend on consumer items. You won't get it by osmosis from New Zealanders.

I found this from the Reserve Bank:

> By mid-2006 the outstanding debt of households had increased around five times in dollar terms since 1990, more than doubling as a percentage of households' disposable income. Weighted average interest rates however had fallen from over 15% to about 8.5% per annum (over 90% of household debt is housing debt, at an average rate of around 8%). Interest servicing of the increased debt, as a percentage of incomes, was about a third higher than in 1990. At current levels, the ratio of household debt to income (excluding student loans) is similar to those found in Australia, the UK and USA.

What does this mean (in English)?

- Well, firstly, Kiwis have bigger mortgages than they used to.
- Mortgages account for 90% of all the household debt (that includes mortgages on rental houses).
- Kiwis pay more interest than they used to (even if interest rates have dropped from 15% to 8.5%)
- There is no difference in debt levels between New Zealand and the UK.

As of 2008, there is a global "Credit Crunch" which is threatening to make life uncomfortable for everyone, whether in New Zealand or not. Questions are being asked: are we going into a period of "Negative Growth"? (Why they can't just say loss I have no idea. I ask you!) Are house prices going to plummet and we all lose our shirts? Should we get out of the share market as it is crashing? Can we hibernate under a thick winter duvet till it's all over?

Well, while most of the economists are in fact saying it's all doom and gloom, some are in fact saying there is no problem: it's a small blip and if everyone just stopped panicking it would all be ok. Who to believe? 😩

I haven't the faintest idea. I also believe that they don't know either. The articles I'm reading are so contradictory that I'm getting whiplash from reading them! So you know what I'm doing? Same as before: I manage our income, ensure we save for our future and get our mortgage paid off as fast as we can.

I'm not worried if house values drop when I think about our home, because whether or not the value of this goes down; we still need a roof over our heads, and as long as I can afford the mortgage, that is all I need to worry about. I've overpaid on the mortgage for a few years, I didn't overextend and get a bigger mortgage than I could comfortably afford to pay, and that cushions me quite a bit when rates go up.

With the rentals we are buying, we do have to be a bit more careful. In this case, I won't buy a property unless I can get it for a much lower price than I would pay if I were buying it as a home. That gives me some leeway if house prices do drop. I also fix the interest rate for as long as possible, so if rates do keep rising, I'm protected for a few years.

Now, something I want to show you; what about house prices going down? What do you see when you look at this graph?

House prices sometimes fall

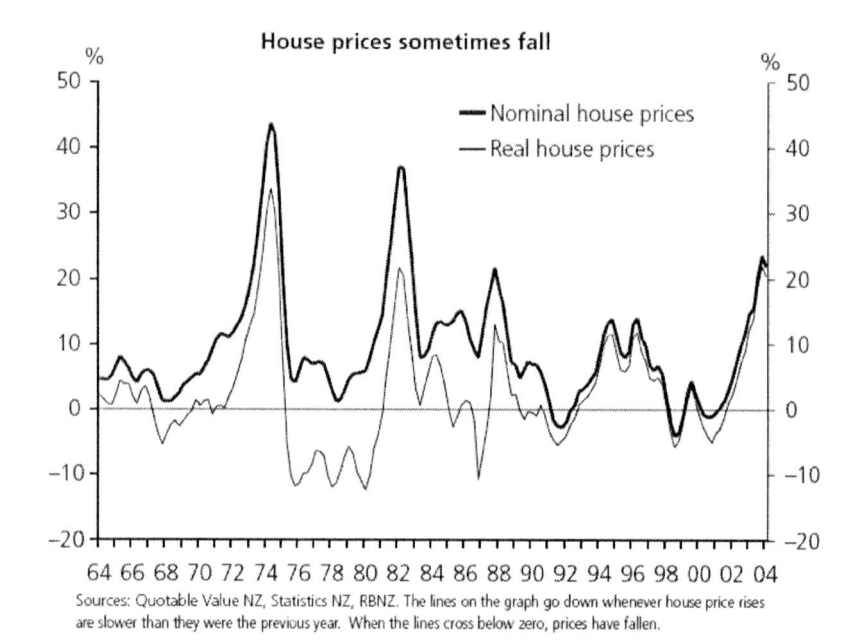

[Graph showing nominal house prices and real house prices from 1964 to 2004, with percentage change on y-axis ranging from -20% to 50%. Sources: Quotable Value NZ, Statistics NZ, RBNZ. The lines on the graph go down whenever house price rises are slower than they were the previous year. When the lines cross below zero, prices have fallen.]

Ask the questions:

- How many years have house prices gone down?
- How many years have house prices gone up?
- How many years have house prices stayed the same?
- What is the difference between nominal and real house prices?

Most people do not actually see what the graph is showing. Most people look at that graph and see that house prices go up and down all the time, and that some of the drops in house prices are horrendous. Just look at 1974 - 1975 😱. But just hang on a minute. Did houses prices really drop in 1975? Nope. In fact – that graph shows quite clearly that house prices in fact still went up in 1975. They just didn't go up very much! The trick is to actually notice the numbers on the side of the graph. Even though there are some really big peaks and troughs in the graph, the troughs don't very often go below zero.

The graph is showing the **percentage increase** in house prices. It is **not** showing house prices themselves. When the line goes below zero, then and only then are house prices falling. If the line stays above zero, then house prices are still going up. I also think it's interesting that looking at the line, when house prices go up, they can reach between 10% and 40% increases in a year quite a lot. When house prices go down, they only ever seem to drop by less than 10%. (If you look at the Real prices).

What is the difference between Nominal and Real House prices? You know, this is one of those things that I think the economists put in so we think we are too stupid to understand. Nominal means the price the house actually sold for, or would have sold for it was for sale. So if you bought a house for $200,000 and 12 months later it was worth $250,000, then the nominal increase is 25%. (50,000 is 25% of $200,000)

The Real value takes into account inflation. So if inflation that year is still at 3%, then the real increase in the house value is only 22%. The same happens when house prices do drop. So between 1976 and 1980, while house prices actually rose slightly; i.e., people had to pay slightly more for a house one year than they would have done the year before, because of inflation, the value was effectively less.

So, when you read articles and look at illustrations telling you what the economy is doing; take a moment to **actually** read the illustrations. Take another moment to read what the article is **actually** saying – if you take out all the hyped-up reporting. They might not always say what the writer tells you it says! The rule I now have is to not believe the headlines. They are usually nothing to do with the **actual** news.

MAKING THE MOVE – GETTING YOUR BUTT (AND MONEY) TO NEW ZEALAND.

Bite off more than you can chew, then chew it.
Plan more than you can do, then do it.
Anon

So you know you really do want to go to New Zealand. You know about the differences, and you are prepared to deal with them. You have done as much homework as it is possible to do, and let's face it, till you actually get yourselves over here, this is still just a book, and still just my opinion.

So, what are the other nuts and bolts you need to take care of when you actually come over here?

CAN I OPEN A NEW ZEALAND BANK ACCOUNT BEFORE I LEAVE THE UK?

*A Bank is a place that will lend you money
If you can prove that you don't need it.*
Bob Hope

Yep! It's fairly easy actually with some banks. Most people I've met have done this with the ASB Bank. In that case you open an account with The Commonwealth Bank Of Australia (which actually owns the ASB), through their London branch.

Commonwealth Bank of Australia
Financial and Migrant Information Service
Senator House
85 Queen Victoria Street
London EC4V 4HA
England
Phone: 44 (0)207 710 3592

It's simply a matter of filling in a form, and sending them ID. Be aware though, that if they offer to move funds to your new account – it can cost you £15 if you are moving less than £30,000 – so you are actually better saying "Thanks, but no thanks" and using a company such as HiFX, or your own favourite currency trader.

You do need to know that you may have bank charges to pay, even if you are not using the account so check this out first and work out how you want to deal with it. If you do not put some funds into the new account, you could end up being overdrawn because of monthly fees, and then get slammed with overdraft fees and interest on top. 😊 In most cases, you will only want a savings account to start with, because there are usually no fees for savings accounts in New Zealand. If you wish to open a current account, then ask the bank which account has no fees. You can always change the account as soon as you get here. Despite the New Zealand banking system's odd rules and regulations, changing accounts is usually simply a matter of a phone call or email to your manager.

Opening up the account from the UK just gives you one less thing to worry about the day you arrive in New Zealand. My mum and dad actually opened up their New Zealand account before they came on their look-see trip. So don't think you have to be ready to actually emigrate in order to do this. Make sure that you get the bank to register you as a Non-Resident for tax, and you will only pay 10% tax on your interest. Don't forget that as soon as you get here as a resident, that you need to apply for your IRD number and get it to the bank as soon as possible, otherwise your tax on any interest shoots up to a whopping 45%, which can hurt – a lot.

You should be offered a "Migrant Banking Officer" when you first arrive, and the idea of this is to help you through the banking system and explain things. They will be your "Personal Relationship manager" for a while however my feeling is that it's better to find someone in a local branch and get them to take over your account as soon as you can.

When you do arrive you will need to pop into a local branch where you can pick up all your cards. You will need an Eftpos card to access your current account and savings account and use the ATM. Unlike in the UK, where it can take up to 10 days to get sent a new card- here you just pop into a branch, they grab a card, swipe it through a machine and get you to load a PIN of your choice on it, and away you go. This speed is basically because your card does not have your name on it; only your Credit Card will have that. If you are offered a credit card (and you may well be), that gets sent to you in the post later.

Your Eftpos card cannot be used like a Switch / Maestro / debit card over the phone or the Internet. You may find this a bit annoying. In order to shop via the phone or Internet, you either need to be able to access Internet banking and set up a payment from your account that way (that's like using the ASB fastcheque), or you need a Credit Card. Incidentally – Westpac has recently brought out a UK style Debit Card – which you **can** use in the same way as we are used to ☺. This also means that if you travel back to the UK on holiday – you can use it to pay for things direct from your New Zealand bank account if you don't have a credit card. You cannot do that with a normal Eftpos card. You can only use a New Zealand Eftpos card to withdraw cash from an overseas ATM (at a cost of $5 a pop), not to buy things in a shop overseas.

And yes, you may well be offered a credit card straight away. Some people appear to need to be in the country a while and proving an income before they get one, but some people get them straight away. Lack of a New Zealand credit history does not seem to be a problem. Remember that you will most likely be charged a fee every 6 months for any credit card you get, and remember also that the rewards schemes are also charged for.

Reward schemes: friend or foe?

I'm not a huge fan of reward schemes in general, because they exist mainly to make people spend more money in the belief that it is better to pay a bit extra and get some points towards a "free toaster". Now, by all means, join as many reward schemes as you want to, just be aware that it is hardly ever worth buying something from a specific shop just to get the rewards. More often than not you would be much better off buying the item from a different shop and getting it cheaper. Then you can use the money saved to buy the toaster anyway.

Fly Buys is the most common reward scheme in New Zealand. So called because you can swap your fly buys points for Air New Zealand Airpoints; and therefore get "free flights". Incidentally you can also use ASB's True Rewards and BNZ's GlobalPlus card to do the same thing.

So let's just look at this a minute. If you collect 300 Fly Buys Points, you can covert that to $50 worth of Airpoints. Which sounds pretty good. But hang on a minute: if you collect your Fly Buys at New World supermarkets, you get 1 fly buy for every $25 spent. So to get 300 Fly buys, or $50 Airpoints, you have to spend $7,500. The question you may want to ask is: Could I shop for less than $7,500 by going elsewhere, and save more than $50, which could then go into a savings account to pay for flights. If it's cheaper to shop elsewhere, and it doesn't inconvenience you to do so (no point driving 50Km to save $5.00) then think carefully about shopping at a particular store in order to get the points.

With ASB's True Rewards, you get a True Rewards Dollar for every $150 you spend on your credit card. So to get the same $50 to spend on flights, you again need to spend $7,500. In this case though, you also have to bear in mind that it can cost you about $40 every six months just to own the card, and another $10 to join the True Rewards system, and you have to pay a $10 fee to convert your rewards to Airpoints. We use our rewards to pay our fees and membership. We have just spent $75 of our True Rewards to cover that, which accounts for $11,250 worth of spending on the credit card. This is before we can accumulate any points for a flippin' stick blender.

Now to clear up a common misconception – the National Bank in New Zealand has the old Lloyds horse as it symbol. However it is **not** part of the UK Lloyds TSB group, and you cannot open an account here in New Zealand through Lloyds TSB if you have an account with them. You used to be able to, but they sold the New Zealand Company to the Australians, and now you can't. Similarly, there is a bank called the TSB here, but that stands for Taranaki Savings Bank, and you can't open an account through Lloyds TSB in the UK. ☻

On the other hand – you **should** be able to open an account with HSBC in New Zealand if you have either a UK HSBC account or indeed a First Direct account. However when we tried this, we got the verbal equivalent of a blank stare from HSBC in the UK. So if you want to try it: good luck with that! You also need to know that HSBC only has branches in Auckland currently, and while you can access your HSBC accounts through the Westpac branches, you apparently need to send all forms to Auckland when opening accounts such as mortgages. I thought this was particularly unhelpful. Apparently the advert that says "Worldwide bank – local knowledge" has yet to filter down to New Zealand.

Out of interest – the four main banks are owned by Australian companies. Sad but true. Kiwibank is the 5th biggest bank in New Zealand and is actually owned by the New Zealand Post Office, not the Australians! Kiwibank seems to have a reputation that is improving all the time, and also seems to have very good interest rates on mortgages, and low fee products. They are advertising heavily these days on the basis that money you spend with them stays in New Zealand rather than being shipped off to Australia as profits. I think it could be well worth looking into. However I have to say that I took them off my list of banks to deal with when I was investigating my mortgage as they just weren't helpful.

HOW DO I RUN MY UK BANK ACCOUNTS FROM NEW ZEALAND?

Create a definite plan for carrying out your desire and begin at once, whether you are ready or not, to put this plan into action.
Napoleon Hill

You really do need to plan for this a bit before you leave the UK. Let's face it: if something goes wrong with your UK account, you can't exactly pop into the local branch (if such a thing still exists these days) and get it sorted out. And if you have a bank with a call centre outsourced to India and you thought it was a nightmare having to explain where Weston-Super-Mare was, just wait till you have to explain your presence in Whangarei! (That's Fong – a – ray by the way, not Wang – er – ry as I first thought).

It's also worth knowing that you probably can't open a UK account once you are no longer resident in the UK, so if you want to be able to change bank accounts – get it done **before** you leave. And check that you can still run them as well as before when you get to New Zealand. Some banks may not even let you keep the account though it appears most of the major ones do.

To my way of thinking you really need to be able to access good Internet banking. It can be faff and hassle to have to wait till 9pm before you can talk to the bank, and most "24 hour phone banking" doesn't actually give you full access, but only allows you to do some of the things you may need to do over the phone.

No matter what you do, chat to your bank before hand and know how much of a service you are still going to get. We have kept our bank account with First Direct – which really is open 24/7 – and every single day of the year. I have had cause to ring them during the night at Christmas, and I really did get to speak to a human being, who was really lovely to deal with even though they had to work on Christmas day. While the customer service has been less than perfect lately they are still a stunningly helpful bank.

Besides you get a special international number to ring, which means you don't end up waiting around, and you get to talk to someone from back home – who will almost always want to know how your new life is going and why you aren't at the beach surfing. 😊 It's a nice touch – and stops banking being stuffy. There are still a few things you cannot do over the phone during the New Zealand daytime, such as sort out problems with your Visa Cards, but on the whole I have found the service to be just as good from over here as it was in the UK. The Internet banking system at First Direct works very well too, so you can operate the account pretty much over the Internet anyway. Also, their cards are black – which I think is quite cool!

So just bear this in mind:

- Can your bank cope with you being 11-13 hours ahead of them?
- Can you cope with running your account with that difference as well?
- Can you access funds in your UK account via your cash card in a New Zealand ATM without incurring charges?
    - If there are charges, what are they, and are you happy with that?

- Could you get a better deal by changing banks?
- Check out www.moneysavingexpert.com for up to date lists on bank charges for using your UK cards overseas.
* Can you control your accounts fully via the Internet?
* Do you **need** a UK bank account?
    - You may need one if you still have bills you need to pay in the UK – some companies will only accept payments from UK Sterling bank accounts.
* Would you be better off having an Offshore Sterling bank account?
    - You usually need minimum balances of at least £2,500 in offshore accounts.
    - Check out www.moneyfacts.co.uk for lists of offshore accounts and current rates.

You should also make sure that you fill in a NORD form for your UK accounts once you become a New Zealand Tax Resident. This means "Not Ordinarily Resident Declaration". Which means that all of a sudden, the UK Inland Revenue won't take tax from the Interest on your savings. Which is cool.

And something which is vitally important: once you have closed down all your utilities in the UK, like gas, electricity, internet, and you have told them not to take any more money from you via Direct Debits – **also tell your bank**! You should always cancel your Direct Debits with the bank, and then if any company "forgets" that they shouldn't be charging you anymore, they can't get your money.

HOW DO I MOVE ALL MY £ TO MY NEW COUNTRY?

It will not do to leave a live dragon out of your plans if you live near one.
J.R.R.Tolkien
The Hobbit

Well, I found the whole concept a bit daunting at first. Currency trading for me was up there with share market trading in the realms of things that economics graduates are supposed to understand. How on earth was I supposed to work out the best time to move my funds to New Zealand? The only currency exchange I had ever done before was buying travelers cheques for a few holidays. And to be honest, we haven't done that too much lately because more and more places have ATM's that we just access our cash from. It's a whole new ball game when you have to move thousands of pounds.

Because we got caught with the exchange rate in the floor at the time we had to buy our house, it was all a bit depressing. We only brought over the minimum to start with, and then brought over the absolute minimum to buy the house with. We kept some funds in the UK to pay our insurance premiums and endowment policy over there.

First of all, why do we need to concern ourselves with exchange rates? Well, here is a quick (and depressing) look at why you need to be able to maximize your money when you convert it.

When we bought our New Zealand home, we paid $595,000 for it. Mum and dad paid $200,000 of that in cash, which they had to move over from the UK, and we paid $135,000 in cash, which we had to transfer as well. The rest we took out a mortgage for. In an ideal world, we could have transferred our funds at a respectable $3 to the £UK. At which point, our home would have cost us the equivalent of just over £198,000. Unfortunately, when we transferred the money, the rate was nearer $2.50 to the £UK. Which meant out home actually cost us the equivalent of £238,000. (That's an extra 20%)

Looking at it another way, the £54,000 we had to bring over as a deposit which gave us $135,000, would have given us $162,000 if the rate had been $3, which would have meant we only needed a $233,000 mortgage instead of a $265,000 mortgage. It's just too upsetting to work out the effect of that on our long-term mortgage interest payments.

So, when you want to move funds from the UK to New Zealand, you have to take into account a few things:

- What is the exchange rate?
- What fees do you have to pay to move your money?
- What is the process you have to go through?

I use a company called HiFX (www.hifx.co.nz or www.hifx.co.uk) to do all my money transfers. I have found that they are really excellent for explaining what to do without making me feel like an idiot for not getting it the first time. There are no extra charges to pay with them either: no flat fee, payment fees, electronic transfer fees or fees to pay to your New Zealand bank for the privilege of putting money in. They do make a profit but it's on the difference between the rate they give you, and the rate they buy at, which is really no different to any other "shop" you buy things from, its just in this case you are buying money.

So when you ask for a quote (for example "I want to send £10,000 to New Zealand") they tell you the rate and what you will get for it at the other end "The rate is 2.9000 and you will get $29,000" (in my dreams!) It really is that easy. They will probably have bought the currency for about 2.93, so make a profit of about 3c for every pound you exchange. With some other companies, you have to take into account fees that they charge at various stages and also sometimes fees that your banks on other end of the deal may charge.

When I want to make a transfer of UK funds to New Zealand dollars:

1. I ring up HiFX and ask for a quote.
2. I tell them how much money I want to move, and which currencies I'm talking about
3. They tell me the rate they can give me, and how much that means I get at the end.
4. We set a "Value Date". This is the date at which I have to have paid my UK funds to HiFX, and they will pay me the New Zealand funds.
5. If I decide to go ahead with the trade, they then send me a confirmation email.

    Note: The verbal agreement is a binding contract and is recorded. The email is simply a confirmation of the contract. If you are unsure about your trade, then do not agree to it over the

phone, and have a think about it. Ask more questions if you have to.
6. I have to fill in the confirmation note with my New Zealand bank account details so they know where to send the money.
7. I then set up an Internet banking payment, to pay HiFX the £UK that I want to transfer. This goes to a HiFX account in the UK
8. The funds turn up a few days later in my New Zealand bank account.

Like this:

> Your UK account → HiFX UK account → your NZ account.

If you need to send money back to the UK for any reason – it just goes the other way:

> Your NZ account → HiFX NZ account → your UK account.

This type of Money Transfer is called a **Spot Trade**. That means that you ring up for the rate, and decide there and then to make the trade. Whatever happens (and again this is what I know of HiFX only), you will be told when you get your quote and agree to the trade **exactly** how much money will hit your New Zealand account. With some other companies, and especially if you deal with the banks, then you have to work that out yourself, by taking into account all the fees.

HiFX is such a simple and friendly company to deal with, that I don't even think of dealing with anyone else now. Once you have done this the first time you really won't think of it as daunting – in fact the only thing you will have to worry about is the actual rate!

HiFX have a minimum amount you can sell in a spot trade: £5,000 or $10,000 if you are selling New Zealand dollars.

There are actually other types of Currency Trade that you can opt for if it's more convenient for you:

Forward Orders
Basically this is a "buy now, pay later" option. If you see a really good rate, and want to "lock it in" but don't want to actually move your money yet, this is a way to do it. You need to be able to set a date at which you will buy the currency. You also need to pay an up-front deposit of 10%. You pay the rest on the set date, and the trade occurs then.

As with the Spot Trade, there is a minimum £5,000 trade.

Market Orders
This is where you can set the rate that you want to exchange at with your trading company. Their systems automatically monitor the rates, and as soon as your chosen rate is achieved, the trade is actioned. You can cancel the order at any time up until the trade has occurred.

The minimum transfer for a market order is £20,000.

Exchange Rate Guarantee
If the exchange rate is really good, and you would like to set a Forward Order, but do not have the funds available to pay a 10% deposit, you can ask for an Exchange Rate Guarantee. You still need to pay a premium up front, but it's much less than 10% (especially if you want to move large sums of money!) Also, unlike with a Forward Order, you are not

actually obliged to go through with the trade if the rate has since improved and you could get a better rate. If the rate improves by the time you want to exchange, you let the contract lapse and make a Spot Order trade. You will lose your premium, but if the rate improves enough, that may not matter to you.

The amount of premium you pay is dependent on a whole load of different factors, so has to be asked for at the time. You also need to be moving a lot of money for this: the equivalent of $100,000 (US $). Not for the faint-hearted, and certainly not for me any time soon!

Regular Payments Service
HiFX also offer a service where you can set up regular payments from the UK to New Zealand (or vise versa).

From the UK to New Zealand:

The minimum amount is £500 per month, you form a contract for 6-18 months and the rate you get is fixed at the start of the contract. So you know exactly how many $$$ you will be getting in your New Zealand account. You set up a Direct Debit from your UK account to the HiFX UK account. Money hits your New Zealand account about 5 days later. Still no extra charges 😊

From New Zealand to the UK

Same deal but the minimum is $1,000 per month.

Please do note though – that HiFX **do not give good** rates when making these monthly payments. In this case, you pay extra in the exchange rate for the convenience of making small monthly exchanges. However, if you know that you will have to send money back to the UK regularly, it is worth having a chat to HiFX and seeing if this is a suitable way for you to do it. The problem with having to send money back is the same as when you bring it over, because exchange rates can be so changeable, you have no idea how much it is going to cost on any given day. This way you get some certainty; but at the cost of good rates.

We are now in the position where we do have to top up our UK bank accounts. Fortunately for us (though I'm pretty sure you would not be happy about now) the exchange rate is even worse than when we brought our funds over to buy the house. Which is good for us, when we have to send money back. We do this in lump sums, as spot orders which means we have a minimum of $10,000 we have to transfer at any one time.

If you don't want to try just HiFX, then it's worth registering with a few money transfer companies (should be free, if not don't touch them), and then when you want to transfer funds for the first time, ask all of them for a quote. Remember: get not only the rate but also the total amount in $ that you get at the end. Then take off any fees that are going to be charged at the UK end, and New Zealand end. Go with the one that gives you the most $$$$ for the least amount of hassle. It's also worth asking your UK bank for their exchange rates and fees, and comparing that as well. This is what I did the first few times – but as HiFX always had the best rate and the best staff – I don't bother with any other company now.

Whoever you use, you will need to set up a trading account, unless you are doing your transfers through the banks. One thing we did find is that with HiFX, you need a trading account in the UK if you live there, and you need another trading account with their New Zealand branch once you move here.

If you think you may need to transfer small amounts, then it is worth looking at your bank account options before you leave the UK. If you have a Nationwide account for example, you can use your ATM card to withdraw $NZ here with no fee charged to your UK account. This is useful when your first arrive. You are then only limited by the amount of funds that your UK bank will let you withdraw from an ATM in one day. Unfortunately, we didn't know this, and our bank, as good as they are, charge us if we want to withdraw funds from foreign ATM's. 😳 Moneysavingexpert.com has up to date information on which banks charge fees for ATM withdrawals and card use abroad.

As for getting used to the whole exchange rate changes thing: well, all I can suggest is that you get used to looking at the rate on the Internet. As soon as you decide you want to head over here, then look for a few sites on the web that track exchange rates. I actually use 2 sites: HiFX, which actually shows the changes in real time, so you can watch (sometimes with mounting horror, and sometimes with unrestrained glee) as the rate changes throughout the day. I also use www.x-rates.com (don't worry, it's honestly a website about exchange rates), which just gives the end-of-the-day exchange rates. This is also the site I use to do any currency conversion calculations. I find it a bit easier to use than the HiFX website, but not as accurate. So if I want a rough idea then I use X-rates, but when I know I'm going to be moving funds, then I tend to watch the HiFX site like a hawk.

The only other thing that I think you need to consider is how much you want to transfer at any one time. You can get better rates if you transfer large sums of money; which you may want to do if you are moving the funds from a UK house sale. However, it really depends on too many factors to say how much you would have to transfer in order to get a better rate. The best thing to do is to ask at the time; what rate could you get if you transferred £5,000, £20,000 or maybe £100,000. We have always transferred small amounts (often the £5,000 minimum) so that we can take advantage of any slight increase in rates. (Let's face it; at the time we needed to move money over, we would take any increase we could get!)

One warning: you can easily get very "het-up" over the exchange rate. Let's face it – the difference between the rates being at $2.50 and $3 is actually huge when you are emigrating and moving potentially large sums of money in order to start you new life. This is especially so when you need that money to buy a house with, and like us, a low rate drastically impacts on the size of mortgage you are then saddled with. I've personally not found any way to deal with the angst of needing to get a higher rate than is available. But recently, as we have been moving money the other way, and the rate kept dropping and dropping; I found that I just had to stop watching at some point and decide that **this** was the rate I was **happy** with and trade. **I then stopped watching the rate**.

I won't look at it again till I'm ready to think about moving funds. You see, having moved the money – if the rate changes and I could have done better – it's too late to do owt about it. So I don't look, and I don't tie myself in knots panicking about the fact that I could have got a few extra bucks. If you are happy exchanging funds at any given rate – that is what is important – not what anyone else thinks you should have exchanged at.

SHOULD I WORK WITH $ OR £ ?

"Since we decided a few weeks ago to adopt the leaf as legal tender, we have, of course, all become immensely rich."
Douglas Adams
The Hitchhikers Guide To The Galaxy

I did both!

I work in $ for the most part, that is I budget in $, and work out costs as a proportion of salary in $. This I think is really important especially when looking at possible mortgages or rents, overall food bills etc. The sooner you get out of the habit of thinking in £ - the sooner you will settle. It took me a long time and I truly believe it was one of the biggest barriers to feeling at home in New Zealand.

Where I continue to convert, is when I want to determine whether or not I think something is worth the money being asked for it. For example: books. Paperback novels retail at around $25 here. Unfortunately even after 12 months - it really didn't mean that much to me, however if I converted it: £10 was a hell of a lot of money to pay for a book! 😲 The shock is even worse when you notice that the UK cover price is still visible on the back and it says £7.99. So I realised that I was being overcharged and popped to Amazon for a better price (where if you buy a few books at a time, you can get them cheaper overall even taking into account the postage). Even at this stage – over three years later and utterly content with my life here, I still find it helpful sometimes to work out a price in

£ to see if it's worth it. I honestly do not know why I cannot determine an item's worth based on the $NZ value. 😯

I also convert when doing price comparisons for online shopping - putting all currencies into £ - so for example if I'm looking at novels (which I do a lot!) I'll go on amazon.co.uk, and amazon.com and compare the prices in £ to what it would cost me in $. This is when I find the Currency Calculator on www.x-rates.com comes in really handy. I really don't know what my problem is; but I just can't seem to understand the relative costs of things unless I know what it costs in £UK. I take my hat off to those migrants who land here and couldn't give a stuff what something would cost if you were in the UK.

Another problem I have (obviously I'm a bit dense when it comes to currencies 😯) is that when I'm in the supermarket and the bill hits $200 I nearly have a heart attack! Every time I hear it - I think its £200! And I still need to do the numbers and say to myself - hey that's only £80 - not to bad for a big shop at all! I still do this even now. I'm sure the staff in the shops think I'm nuts.

Generally - I agree with the majority of migrants in that you should try and work in $NZ, but if like me you can't get your head round whether $100 is cheap or expensive for a given item, convert to £UK so that it does make sense to you. The sooner you learn to work in $ - the better. It's just taken me a long time.

By the way; I do not think that having a problem getting your head round whether something is a good price or not, and struggling to come to terms with a new currency, in anyway makes you a "bad migrant". Least ways, I feel I am pretty successful as a migrant, and I'm very settled in my life here.

Having a minor coronary in the supermarket does not make me an abject failure in my new life; and it won't make you one either! My best advice is try to get used to the fact that you earn dollars and spend in dollars, and that at the end of the day, it is really mostly irrelevant what it would cost you if you were in the UK, because you are not in the UK now.

If you end up like me, and struggle with it – then please do not worry about it. The sky will not fall on you, and you will not be frog-marched back to the UK in disgrace.

I'M LEAVING THE UK – IS MY PENSION COMING WITH ME?

*You **can** have it all.*
You just can't have it all at once.
Oprah Winfrey

You may have heard, or even seen adverts – which tell you that you can cash in your UK pension because you are emigrating. Weyhey! 😊 All of a sudden – you don't have to wait till you retire to get your mitts on the cash!

Before you get too exited – not that I want to rain on anyone's parade – but its not **quite** that simple. Basically – you can if you want to move your UK pension over to a New Zealand Superannuation scheme – as long as the New Zealand scheme is "Approved" by the Inland Revenue in the UK. Your chosen New Zealand scheme should have QROPS status (Qualifying Recognised Overseas Pension Scheme). That's not too much of an issue: all the companies doing transfers should have registered their schemes for this, and you should get some choice in what your pension pot gets invested in over here. However – you can no longer cash in the pension once you get it over here 😊.

Moving your pension is relatively easy to do – you can either ask your New Zealand bank to do it for you (most banks have their own investment people who can help you out), or you can use a specialist company – that spends all day every day rescuing peoples pension funds.

You may have to pay a fee. (There's a surprise!) For us it was 5% of the value of the pension (which can **really** hurt if you have been very good and saved a lot), or a minimum fee of $500 – if you have not been quite so diligent (like me in this case). Some companies charge a sliding scale of fees depending on the size of the pot to be transferred, such as Lyfords (www.uk-pension-transfer.co.nz). Some of the banks may do the transfer for free, but bear in mind that they will only do that to stick it in their own pension funds – so you will be limiting your choices. You really need to shop around.

Now, the thing is that due to a change of rules in the UK during 2006, transferring your pension could be a little less attractive in some ways, than it was when we did this. We were able to cash in the whole of some of the pensions (they were my personal pension because I had been so bad at saving that they were not worth much), and 49% of my husbands pension (he was a lot better at saving than me in those days).

Now, there is a huge amount of confusion about the new rules (and to be honest – most of us had enough trouble getting our heads round the old rules). So here are the basics:

- You have to transfer your pension from a UK Pension Scheme to a New Zealand superannuation Scheme.
- You cannot transfer your pension straight into a bank account (unfortunately).
- You should make sure the transfer is to a QROPS registered scheme.
    - If it isn't – you will be taxed in the UK at up to 55% of the value of your fund.

- You can find a list of QROPS funds at www.hmrc.gov.uk/pensionschemes/index.htm - click on List of QROPS
- Your New Zealand Scheme provider is obliged to tell the UK Inland Revenue if you withdraw any funds from your scheme in the first 5 years.
    - You can be liable in this case for **up to 55% tax** on the money you take out 😱.
- You cannot access the funds until you are 55 years old (this is the UK Inland Revenue rule – your New Zealand Scheme may have rules meaning you cannot access the fund until later in life)
- You must have New Zealand residency to be able to transfer your superannuation fund.
- You cannot transfer your pension from the UK once you have started drawing it.
- Bear in mind that in New Zealand, superannuation schemes are taxed as they grow.
- Even if you don't transfer your pension – you may be taxed on the growth in your fund in the UK, either by the UK or the New Zealand tax office.
    - This is because New Zealand now taxes growth on Foreign Investments (and a UK pension counts).
    - Your UK pension could be exempt from this if you do not pay any more contributions into it.

When using a company to do the transfer it's all rather hands off and easy. With Britannia (the company we used) for example, someone came to our house and spent quite a bit of time explaining the process (not that well to be honest). He took some information, which basically allowed him to get "quotes" from our UK Pension Providers. There should be no fee for this; in fact you shouldn't have to pay anything to anyone until the transfer is successfully completed.

Once we had the quote that was the point at which we had to decide whether to go ahead or not. We personally felt that Britannia were not a great company to deal with. They took an inordinately long time to get anything done, and were less than helpful at explaining to us why there were delays. When they did talk to us; they told us we had caused the delay by not getting paperwork to them.

The thing was I wanted to know what was happening **after** they got the paperwork, being fully aware that we had not signed the requisite paperwork immediately. The problem was that Britannia does not want you phoning your UK pension companies to find out what is going on. From my experience, this is because the UK Pension companies are happy to tell you when they received papers from Britannia, and when they actioned it, which leaves you wondering what on earth Britannia are doing in the meantime.

We also found that once the UK pension companies released the funds (they were more than happy to tell us exactly how big the cheque was), Britannia sat on them for an annoyingly long time, and were "unable" to tell us how much we had got for our £UK. As the customer, we had absolutely no control over when the funds were banked by Britannia, or when they released them to us. It took more argy bargy than it should have done for someone to tell me how much the funds were worth. Lyfords on the other hand now have access to funds in New Zealand that operate in £UK, so if the exchange rate is pretty appalling – you have the option of keeping the fund in £UK and then swapping to a $NZ when the rate improves. Which is neat!

On the positive side; we did get the cash eventually. We ended up with about $19,000 which had to stay in a New Zealand superannuation scheme (51% of one of my Husband's pensions), and about $18,000 in cash which we could take from that scheme. We also ended up with $14,000 in cash from my pensions. If we were to do this now, of course, all of the funds would end up in a new Superannuation Scheme.

Wehyey 😃 So did we spend up?

Hell no! We used a chunk of the money to pay down our mortgage. We also used some to build up our emergency fund. I try whenever possible not to divert money that we have saved for the future into money we spend now. So the way I saw it, was that although we were cashing out our pensions, we had to ensure that whatever we did with that money – it would not have a negative impact on our future. One way or another, it had to work for us. Paying off some of our mortgage was the most cost effective use of it. Although the emergency fund can in theory be spent (if we have an emergency), while the emergency does not come calling, the money sits in our revolving credit account and works all the time to lower our interest payments.

So, are there reasons why it's worth transferring your pension, and equally, are there reasons not to do it? Personally I think it is less clear-cut now that you cannot cash in the pension without a huge tax penalty. The biggest reason to transfer now is that when you actually get to retirement age, you can withdraw the whole of your fund tax-free. Whereas if you leave it in the UK and draw on it – you can only take out a proportion of it as a tax-free lump sum, and you will be taxed in New Zealand on the income you get from the rest of it.

> ### Pension vs. Superannuation
>
> Something to be aware of is that with a UK pension, you need to use some of the fund to "buy an annuity". This means that you can take a bit of it as cash – but most of it has to be kept safe, and that will provide you an income until you die.
>
> With a New Zealand Superannuation fund – you can use the fund to live on as you choose. You do not have to keep some of it back, so it's up to you to use the fund wisely and make it last. Once it's gone – it's gone! This applies to Kiwisaver as well.

All in all I think I would still transfer our funds, even though we would not be able to cash them in. For me it just gives a sense of security knowing that our retirement fund is in the same country as me, and that there are no more changes coming to the UK Pension tax laws which could hinder my future plans.

On the other hand, we did leave one of our pensions in the UK alone. This is a pension my husband had with IBM while he worked for them. In that case, there was already a fairly nice amount of money in it, but on top of that, there were also some life insurance benefits with it. Basically, not only does it pay Alan a pension on retirement, but should he die, it pays the pension to me, both as a lump some and an ongoing income. That was the only pension we had that gave us benefits which we felt were worth keeping.

So you really do need to weigh up your options and as ever, work out what is best for you. The great thing about this is that you do not need to decide anything before you come out to New Zealand. So take your time, and leave this on a back burner until you have settled yourself in New Zealand. Once you have worked out that you are staying here, you have got your head round living here, then you can take a look at your pensions! Make sure you get some good advice though – specifically geared to **your needs and circumstances**.

SO WHAT HAPPENS TO OUR UK STATE PENSIONS?

*If you think the government is going to keep you in the
style to which you have become accustomed
once you've retired, think again —
unless you're on the breadline now.*
Gareth Morgan,
Pension Panic

Well, right off the bat, we have to acknowledge that we are now dealing with government agencies, so of course any information you do find is almost impossible for us mere mortals to read and understand.

However, the crux of it is that you cannot move your state pension "fund" out of the UK in the same way that you can move a private pension. So you cannot access any of the money in it early.

What you can do is still claim a UK state pension when you retire in New Zealand. Currently, this is subject to the following rules and conditions:

- If you are currently receiving the UK State Pension, the amount of pension you will get is frozen at the level it is when you become a resident of New Zealand.
- If you emigrate, and then later become eligible for the UK State Pension, the amount is frozen at the level it was when you left the UK.

- Any UK State Pension that you do get will be taken off any New Zealand state Superannuation you may be entitled to.
    - This means that you cannot claim the UK state pension and add it to the New Zealand Superannuation.
- You can continue to contribute to the UK State Pension while you are resident in New Zealand if you wish.
    - Any contributions that you make will increase your UK State Pension.
    - Remember though that any increase you do gain will simply decrease the amount of New Zealand Superannuation you are entitled to.

Now, in order to be eligible to receive the New Zealand Superannuation, you have to have been resident in New Zealand for a total of 10 years since you turned 20. Five of those have to be since you turned 55 years of age.

The New Zealand Superannuation pays out to both men and women when they turn 65.

New Zealand Superannuation payments 2008		
Fortnightly Payment	Before Tax	After Tax (19.5% tax)
Single Living alone	$695.54	$571.74
Single (Shared Living)	$640.22	$527.76
Married / De-facto couple	$528.74 (each)	$439.80 (each)

If you have any other income, then bear in mind that your tax rate may differ from this. For example, if you earned $38,000 from other sources, then your Superannuation would be taxed at 33%, not at 19.5%.

WHAT SHOULD WE DO WITH UK POLICES AND INSURANCES?

> *"Fun is like life insurance;*
> *the older you get, the more it costs."*
> Kin Hubbard

If you are anything at all like me, then thinking of sorting out all your various life insurance policies and whatnots will be the last thing you want to do prior to starting your new life. But it is important.

There is a very big and very important difference between UK and New Zealand insurance policies, and that is in the way premiums are worked out. In the UK, when you buy life insurance, or Critical Illness cover, then the premium is worked out on the basis of your age when you take the policy out. And it stays at that level till the policy pays out, or the term of the policy ends – whichever is sooner. This means that the younger you are when you take out the policy – then the cheaper it is in the long run. My Grandma – who sadly died before we came to New Zealand, was paying the princely sum of £3 a **year** for her life policy by the time she died. In fact the company had stopped taking the money a few years before as it was costing them more to collect than they were actually collecting.

Whereas in New Zealand; no matter what age you take the policy out, the premium can often increase every year – so as you get older – your insurance costs go up, regardless of how old you were when you started the scheme. It appears that not many people hold onto their policies very long here. 😲

So – if you have policies in the UK – it's well worth hanging on to them for dear life if you can. That means that you won't have to worry about a replacement policy getting more expensive every year.

If you choose to get new policies in New Zealand, then be very careful about the type of premiums you pay. We took out a Life Insurance policy here for my husband, with Sovereign, and have ended up with our premiums quoted as "Level – 10 years". That means that the premium we have been quoted will stay the same every month for the next 10 years; which is almost as good as my UK policy (a Term Life Insurance policy which runs for 15 years.) I will soon be looking at changing this with the help of a financial advisor, because it is possible to get the premium set for life!

If you take out a policy where the premiums change every year, then you need to add up the total amount of premiums over the lifetime of the policy you want. You will probably pay substantially less to begin with, but as you start getting older, those premiums tend to get bigger and bigger a lot faster.

I think it's well worth keeping your UK policy going, because even if you can get set premiums on a new New Zealand policy, there's virtually no chance of picking up a policy that will be as cheap as your UK one. That is not because insurances are more expensive in New Zealand (they can be, but ours were fairly similar in cost), but purely because if you took out a policy 5 or 10 years ago, you just cannot get the same cover for the same price now because you are older.

However – you **must** check that your UK policies will cover you if you live in New Zealand. And **please** do not take the word of a help line operator as proof that you are covered. You really do need to write a letter and get a written reply back. The last thing you want in the event of needing to claim is for the company to try and wheedle their way out of paying up. 😒

You will also need to decide whether you want to pay the policy from money you leave in the UK – which is what we have done – or whether you want to pay it from your New Zealand bank account. You will have to bear in mind if you do this – that you are at risk from currency fluctuations. Your £10 premium may be $25 one month or $30 the next month. Some companies may insist that you pay from a UK sterling account. You will need to find this out – because it is one of the things that will decide whether or not you keep your old bank accounts.

And something else we found: you cannot always start a UK policy once you are resident in New Zealand. And even then – you will probably only be allowed to set one up with a company you already deal with. We found that Friends Provident was the only UK company we dealt with that would allow us to get new policies from New Zealand – they even have a special International Sales Department. All our current policies are still in force and happy to cover us, but the other companies would not set up anything new.

Check all your insurance policies to see if they have a "Maximum days Out Of The UK" Clause. This should include checking your travel insurance and medical insurance. If you are hoping that travel or medical insurance will pay any fees if you have a medical problem in the early days of your emigration – you may be disappointed. The policies we had that were affected had a 90-day limit on the amount of time you could be out of the country.

If you feel that you can get away without proper insurance in New Zealand – you are wrong. If you need convincing – then you should read a book called "Cover Your Breasts" by Alison Renfrew.

www.coveryourbreasts.co.nz

Alison has survived recent breast cancer and has written about her experiences. She is also a financial planner and advises people on insurance. Her book, while being a fascinating diary of her fight with cancer, also highlights the dire need for private insurance and not having to rely on the public health system here when things go horribly wrong.

We were absolutely horrified when we arrived here to find that our private medical insurance (Southern Cross) does not cover the cost of Chemotherapy if we get cancer. This is because the public system funds it. Well, yes, they do – eventually. They do not rush these things because they cannot afford to. You do not want to have to wait to start treatment for this! So our choices were either to pay for extra trauma cover, or run back to the UK in the event of cancer and throw ourselves on the NHS! A sobering thought?

Herceptin – a drug for certain types of breast cancer can cost over $120,000 a year. The government will not pay for it in New Zealand for more than 9 weeks. The cost of treating women in New Zealand with Herceptin would take 2.5 times the current total budget for all cancer care, and the government has decided you are on your own ☹.

Can you afford to pay $120,000? Would you have to sell your house? This does not even include all the tests and surgeries you may need. Many of us complain about the NHS waiting lists – just wait till you have to get treatment on the public system here. Our view of it, and we have seen this in action with colleagues – is that the public health system makes you wait long enough that they may not have to bother treating you at all.

Please – get some advice on your health and life cover. You need it and you and your family deserve it. If you feel you do not earn enough to pay for it – then look for a job that pays you enough so that you can afford it.

WHEN SHOULD I APPLY FOR MY NEW ZEALAND TAX NUMBER?

*Of the two classic certainties, death and taxes,
death is preferable.
At least you're not called in six months later for an audit.*
Bill Vaughn

As soon as possible.

The thing is – you will be classed as a "Tax Resident" in New Zealand if you spend more than 183 days a year in the country. While you may be tempted to hold off on getting an IRD number straight away and pay tax on any interest on savings at the "Non Resident" rate of 10% (which admittedly sounds a bit tempting), if you go over the 183 days without having got an IRD number – they class you as a tax resident and whack your tax rate up to 45%. **And** they then backdate that to the day you arrived, whether you were a **resident** or not. Depending on how much money you had sitting in the bank that could really hurt. So unless you know you are only coming for a few months, suck it up and get an IRD number! Never hack off the IRD – it just ain't worth it.

What is the difference between a **Resident** and a Tax Resident?

These are two terms that it is worth knowing the difference between. Because there are forms you may come across that ask if you are a Tax Resident (sometimes written as "Resident for Tax Purposes"), and forms that ask if you are a Resident.

> Basically, you are a **Resident** of New Zealand if you have a Residence Permit in your passport.
>
> You are a Tax Resident if you spend more than 183 days a year in New Zealand.
>
> It is entirely possible to be a Tax Resident without being a Resident. Say, for example, you have a Work Visa for 2 years. Once you have been here for over 6 months, then you are a Tax Resident, but you are not a **Resident** as far as immigration is concerned.

This is going to be important if you enter the country on a Visitors Visa, and end up converting to a Residency Visa. If, like us, you enter on a residency visa straight away, and have a job to go to – it's not really an issue. Just be aware that if you do not have your IRD number when you start the job – you will lose 45% in tax (plus ACC contributions) until such time as you give them a number.

As of February 2008, you can no longer apply for an IRD number until you get to New Zealand. You can however download the forms from the IRD website so that you are ready to apply as soon as you get here.

- www.ird.govt.nz.
- Under Forms And Guides, click on
  IRD number application - individual IR595
- This covers both adults and children.

You will need to send two different documents, which the IRD class as a Category A document and a Category B Document. This means a copy of your UK passport (Category A), and a copy of your drivers license (Category B). The IRD Website currently does not list an overseas drivers license as a suitable Category B Document. However, speaking to them over the phone, they have confirmed that they will accept this.

Send the application to:
>Inland Revenue
>PO Box 3753
>Christchurch

If you need to talk to someone at the IRD about anything – the number to call from the UK is:

- 64 4 978 0779
- Also use this number if calling from New Zealand and you won't get cut off "because we are too busy to answer the phone" – just a tip!

I have found the people there immensely helpful, and they really do explain things very well and in clear English!

Everyone should have an IRD number in New Zealand. This includes children, if they are going to be working, or have New Zealand bank or savings accounts. Partly – this is because children pay tax on savings interest, but also because if you are claiming the "Working for Families" tax credit, you need the IRD numbers for the children in order to do so. So if there is any possibility you may qualify – get the IRD number straight away. Without an IRD number for the child, your "Working for Families" tax credit is stopped after 8 weeks.

DON'T I GET A TAX EXEMPTION FOR FOUR YEARS?

"I'm spending a year dead for tax reasons."
Douglas Adams.

Wow – wouldn't that be sweet. It's not quite that tasty – but if you get your Residence to New Zealand now, (After April 2006 – bit late for me 😞) then you are actually exempt from paying income tax in New Zealand on your **overseas** income. So any earnings you still have from the UK, you don't have to pay tax on in New Zealand.

Now – what you need to know about this;

- The exemption runs for 4 years from the date you become a tax resident in New Zealand.
    - Like the IRD number and tax rate thing – if you don't claim tax residence from day one (e.g., you are on a Visitors Visa to start with) – they will backdate the 4 years to start from the date you entered the country.
- You can only get the exemption once, for 4 years.
- You cannot get the exemption at the same time as claiming "Working for Families" tax credits.
    - So you do need to work out which scenario gives you the most moohlah– time to sit down with a calculator!
- The tax exemption is given automatically – you do not have to apply for it. 😊

- You simply do not have to tell the Inland Revenue about your offshore income (Weyhey – the tax office made something easy!😊)
- Not **all** foreign income is exempt from tax, but most is. Items that you still pay tax on are:
    - Income from work you do abroad while living in New Zealand
    - Income from services that you sell from New Zealand.
    - That means that if you are living here, but you are still employed to do a job in the UK – you are **not** exempt from paying income tax in New Zealand, on the money you earn.

So, what exactly is exempt from New Zealand Income Tax under these rules?

Well, it looks to me like you need a PhD to understand what is exempt from income tax. On the off chance that anyone reading this does in fact have a PhD, here goes:

- Controlled foreign company income that is attributed under New Zealand's Controlled Foreign Company (CFC) rules
- Foreign investment fund income that is attributed under New Zealand's Foreign Investment Fund (FIF) rules (including foreign Superannuation)
- Non-resident withholding tax (for example on foreign mortgages)
- Approved issuer levy (for example on foreign mortgages)
- Income arising from the exercise of foreign employee share options
- Accrual income (from foreign financial arrangements)

- Income from foreign trusts
- Rental income derived offshore
- Foreign dividends
- Foreign interest
- Royalties derived offshore
- Income from employment performed overseas before coming to New Zealand, such as bonus payments
- Gains on sale of property derived offshore (held on revenue account)
- Offshore business income (that is not related to the performance of services).

So mostly it covers income from various types of investments, rental income, bonuses from your old job, and business income along as you sell items and not services (that is: you can sell Widgets by the truck load, you just can't fix Widgets!)

Is that clear?

Personally I get the impression that this is one of those things that sounds really good in principle, but will actually not affect that many migrants. The most useful items are not having to pay tax here in New Zealand on your UK bank interest, and for some migrants, not being taxed if you rent out your UK house rather than selling it. It certainly doesn't look as wonderful as many of us thought when we first heard about the "Tax Exemption".

WILL WE GET WORKING FOR FAMILIES TAX CREDITS?

"For every benefit you receive a tax is levied."
Ralph Waldo Emerson

Working For Families (WFF) is a Family Assistance package to help low-ish income families and is paid to families with children under 18 years. If you find you are entitled to it – then claim it – cos every little helps, and let's face it – you may in fact be earning relatively less than you would like. It could mean the difference between having a successful emigration and going back. **Anything** that helps bring more money in (or more correctly – stops the government nicking as much money off you) is all-good. Bear in mind – WFF is just the government giving you back some of the tax you have already paid – so grab it with both hands. Personally, I would much rather the government just took less tax in the first place, off all of us, but that's just me.

Whether you will be entitled to WFF is dependent on a mix of your family income, and how many children you have. The more children, the more you can earn and still qualify for WFF. Those with fairly high wages need to have a rugby team in order to apply.

Now – you may look this up at the IRD, and see this wonderfully confusing "Eligibility Criteria" – which is almost as bad as some of the stuff NZIS comes out with:

- You must meet **at least one** of the following residency requirements:
    - You are both a New Zealand **resident** and a New Zealand tax resident and have been in New Zealand continuously for at least 12 months at any time.
    - You are caring for a child who is both present and **resident** in New Zealand. (This is Immigration Residency, not tax residency)

Well, being a bit of a numpty sometimes, I was wondering: if only **one** of those has to be the case, why would you ever have to wait one year to be able to apply – because surely as soon as the parent gets residency – the child also has residency. Well, after tying my head in knots for quite a while, and finding out that the Inland Revenue don't really know what it means either – I think I finally worked it out.

My guess is (and it is just a guess) that this would cover you if for some reason you were not a resident yourself, but had the full time care of a child who was a resident. When that would apply I have no idea – but then if it were up to me, I'd have written a rule that made sense!

So – if you have a dependent child who has a Residency Visa and lives here in New Zealand – you can apply for WFF if your income levels make you eligible, and you basically ignore the first point. Clear as mud?

What this does mean – is that you cannot qualify for WFF if you are on a Visitors Visa (when you shouldn't be working anyway!) or on a Work Visa or other temporary visa. It has to be a **Residency Visa**. Sorry.

There are different types of benefits that come under the heading of "Working For Families", and they each have different income limits for eligibility. These are the figures up to March 2008. To see updated figures, check out the WFF website:

www.workingforfamilies.govt.nz/tax-credits

Upper Earnings Limits in order to be Eligible for WFF			
Number Of Children	Maximum Annual Family Income Allowed (Before Tax)		
	Family Tax Credit	In – Work Tax Credit	Parental Tax Credit
1	$56,320	$71,920	$111,027
2	$71,140	$86,740	$125,847
3	$85,960	$101,560	$140,667
4	$100,780	$120,280	$159,387
5	$115,600	$139,000	$178,107
6	$130,420	$157,720	$196,827

Family Tax Credit
Paid to families whether they work for income, or their income comes in the form of other Government Benefits. This is to help with the day-to-day living costs of your family.

In Work Tax Credit
Paid to families if the combined working hours are more than 30 hours, or 20 hours if you are a solo parent.

Parental tax credit
This is paid to cover the first 56 days after a new baby is born. If however you take Paid Parental Leave – which you may be

entitled to after you have worked for the same employer for 6 months – then you cannot claim the Tax Credit – it's one or the other I'm sorry to say.

There is also another WFF tax credit called Minimum family tax credit which is paid in order to bring a working Families income up to a minimum level of $347 a week after tax. Hopefully you will never be in the position of needing this. If any Skilled Migrant is being paid that level of wages there is something wrong with the system somewhere! 😳

HOW MUCH DOES IT ACTUALLY COST TO EMIGRATE?

It takes a lot of money to make these dreams come true.
Walt Disney

A lot.

In fact I think the reason most of us never go back and look at how much we spent to move to New Zealand is because the numbers involved are so big!

So, for starters, below is what we spent in order to start a new life. I have used updated figures for the Immigration forms. You can check the costs for these at www.immigration.govt.nz. I've given the fees for the Skilled Migrant Category – obviously if you emigrating under a different scheme then the fees may be different. The other costs are what we actually spent – these were for a move that occurred in December 2004.

ITEM	COST	NOTES
Immigration forms		
EOI	$400	Online form ($500 for Paper Form)
Medical Assessment	£260	For two of us – done in Carlisle.
VISA	$1,800	Once they want to give you a blue sticker!
Migrant Levy	$300 each	Maximum of $1200 Payable on any application
IRRV (Indefinite Returning Residents Visa)	$100	Apply after 2 years of residence.
Moving Costs		
Shipping	£3,385	A 20ft Container

Extra Shipping Costs	$150	Added on at New Zealand end
Shipping Insurance	£1,390	Paid to shipping company – 3% of value of goods.
Flights	£3,985	2 x one way business class (well why not?)
Car Hire	£335	One week to travel Auckland to Wellington
Holiday Accommodation	£388	Took a week holiday on our way down.
Sky Jump and Zorbing	£145	Start as we mean to go on!
First few weeks accommodation	£834	Staying in the J Street Apartments, Wellington
Look See Trip to New Zealand	£2,830	We spent 3 weeks here, 15 months before arriving as residents (includes flights)
Selling the House	£3,607	Lawyers and Estate agent fees
The Leaving Party	£260	Had to be done
TOTAL NZ$ SPENT	**$3,050**	
TOTAL UK£ SPENT	**£17,419**	

Now obviously, your costs may be different, but at least it gives you some idea of what to expect. You may not want to travel business class; you may not be able to! Our flights were also extra expensive because we had to book last-minute flights over the Christmas holiday – that is just the way the job situation worked out for us. It turned out that it was going to cost a huge amount for us to fly anyway, even if we went economy, and that was if we could get a flight at all! Also, booking business class was not so bad when it was only two of us; it could well be a different story if you have a family to consider as well.

The immigration fees you can do nothing about. The fees are set in stone, and it is either pay the fees, or don't get your visas.

You should always check on the NZIS website for any changes to the fee structure, and look at the Guide To Fees.

You may also need to bear in mind that if you have any medical issues, and your residency application is referred to the Medical Assessor, then you may have costs involved for extra tests. We have found this when applying for residency for my parents. Not only do you have the extra stress and hassle of having to wait longer for your application to be approved – but you have to pay for all the tests out of your own pocket (unless you have a doctor who can get them done on the NHS).

Now, regarding shipping your worldly goods to New Zealand: this is the one bit of your emigration that you must research very carefully. Too many migrants have started out their new life with huge amounts of stress and worry because of shipping companies. So here is what you need to know:

- Often, a different company is sub-contracted to deal with your container when it gets to New Zealand.
- The contract you sign with a shipping company in the UK is a contract with the UK company only.
    - You do not have a contract with the New Zealand subcontractor.
    - That contract is between the UK company and the New Zealand subcontractor.
- Some of the New Zealand companies have been known to slap on large fees, which you have to pay in order to get your goods from them.
    - These are usually in the form of "MAF Inspection Fees".

- These fees can be hundreds of dollars, and bear no relation to the fees that MAF actually charge to the New Zealand company.
- If you do not want to pay the fees (and why the hell should you?) you have a fight on your hands, and often you need to try and get the UK company to fight for you.

This is a horrendous situation, and it is one that the UK shipping companies seem to be well aware of, but won't do anything about. 😡 They also do not warn prospective clients that this may happen, or indeed help their clients when it does happen. I have to say I think it's disgusting. The only way people have generally managed to sort out the mess is by getting help off other migrants on Internet forums who have had the same problems.

So what can you do? Firstly – when you get the quotes from the UK shipping companies: ask them outright whom they will be using on the New Zealand end. You then need to research on the Immigration forums to find out the current companies that you need to avoid at all costs. If your shipping company insists on using those subcontractors – **do not use that company**. It's as simple as that. Until the UK companies tidy up this mess – I do not feel they should get our business.

Most of the time, your shipping contract will not cover your MAF fees, because it's claimed that you can never be certain what the fees will be. I think that's a load of rubbish. For the majority of migrants, the MAF fees are not likely to be exorbitant, and it should be possible to work out a **fair** average fee and add it into the UK bill, rather than having the New Zealand companies hold migrants hostage. Bear in mind that shipping companies do send people round to assess your belongings and give you a quote. Surely they know their jobs well enough by now that they can see if you are likely to require a long and detailed MAF Inspection?

Finally, if your MAF fees are not included in your quote, you can write in that you will pay the MAF fees directly to MAF on production of an Invoice from MAF, and ask the shipping company to sign it before you agree to the contract. It's worth a shot. Do not pay MAF fees to any company that does not provide you with the bill from MAF.

You can actually avoid this issue completely by asking that your container be delivered directly to a New Zealand address, and arranging a MAF inspection direct to your home. You will then be responsible for paying all the MAF fees directly, including any transport costs. This is certainly an option if you wish to avoid all the hassles that some migrants come across.

If you do find that you are having issues with this – then the first thing you need to do is complain (loudly) to the UK Company and tell them you expect them to sort out the mess. You may have to keep going, and try to get to the highest level of management. Do not take this lying down. You can also contact MAF directly and get them to tell you what the inspection fee actually came to. You will need to find that out in order to see just how much the shipping company is adding to your bill. According to MAF – you as the importer are entitled to know what your MAF fees were, and they are happy for you to pay directly as a cash client.

You can contact MAF Biosecurity on
09 909 3030. (00 64 9 909 3030 from the UK)

Make no mistake – **this is a rip off**. 😠 The New Zealand companies get paid by the UK shippers. If they are not charging enough to cover their costs, they shouldn't be coming to us to fill in the gaps, or try and cream extra off the top!

The good news: **Not all companies that subcontract do this** 😊. We actually shipped 2 containers. For the first, we used John Masons. The New Zealand company used was Allied Movers (not the same as Allied Pickfords). We were charged a reasonable $150 in extra fees and MAF fees. When it came time to send the second container, we again contacted John Masons. This time, they were going to use a subcontractor known to cause problems. We spoke to them about it, and they were fully aware of the problem. As they were not prepared to do anything about the situation, we did not use John Mason for the shipping. The rep had the gall to be quite angry! Instead, we used Crown Relocations. This is one of the cases where you use the same company at both ends: Crown has depots in all the major New Zealand cities. We had a few extra fees added, mostly in this case for storage; and again it came to about $150. Some migrants have been charged well over $500 extra in fees, for pretty much the same thing that cost us only $150. If Allied Movers and Crown can offer a fair service – why can't other companies? 😊

You also need to be aware that if you are shipping your goods to New Zealand and you have anything other than a residency visa or a long term work visa (valid for more than 1 year); you have to pay GST on anything you ship. Be warned – as this can be very expensive indeed. According to customs, (which I have to say were not exactly helpful) the GST is worked out on about 50% of the price you paid for the item. It all sounds like a bit of a nightmare to me, so I would be very careful about importing stuff unless you have a long-term visa. You can get a fair idea of rates that are charged by looking on the New Zealand Customs website. The rates charged are different for each type of item; a lot of items are free of charges, many are around 6-7%, and some over 15%.

- Go to www.customs.govt.nz
- Click on Importers, then Private Importers, then Customs Charges.
- If you need to speak to a customs officer about your likely charges – do not ring the National Call Centre. They are not really that wonderful to speak to. Instead, call the office nearest to where you will be living. You can find the numbers on the website above.

Don't skip insurance on your shipping. The chances of your container ship being lost at sea are slim – but this is everything you own we are talking about here. Can you really afford to replace everything if it does go down? You will never be able to replace things like your photos (we scanned all ours and brought the laptop with us on the plane), but it will help you sleep easier to know that you will be able to replace most of it. You need to take note though that most insurance is invalid if you packed your own goods. Bear this in mind if you choose to use the "You Pack, We Ship" type companies. You may save money – but if something goes wrong – you don't have a leg to stand on. While I will vigorously look for cheaper options on a lot of things; when we are talking about getting my whole life packed up and moved round the world; I go for "reassuringly expensive".

Onto more pleasant aspects ☺ – you need to budget for the first few weeks of accommodation in a hotel or motel. I personally would not advise organising a long term rental from the UK, basically because a lot of rental properties are somewhat below the standards you might expect. (And I say that as someone who buys rental properties and is horrified at what a lot of landlords will allow other human beings to live in).

It pays to be on the ground and able to look at what you are going to live in. Pictures on the Internet can be deceptive. We stayed in the J Street Apartments in the Central Business District (CBD) of Wellington. That meant easy access to Hubby for work, and we were right in the heart of the city for transport and looking at our longer-term options. J Street is what's known as an Apartment Hotel, which is very popular here in New Zealand. Basically, you can get one or two bedroom apartments, with separate living areas and a small kitchenette. We found this pretty ideal to start with.

Whatever you do – it is going to be a very expensive journey for most of us. We do have some friends who only had a few boxes of stuff to ship, and basically no other costs on top of that except the flights. So it can be done on the cheap for some people.

I don't advise selling everything up to avoid the shipping costs and then hoping to re-buy everything again when you get over here. It sounds good in theory; but completely ignores just how much it can cost to buy replacements over here, and the fact that you will rarely be able to sell your items for anything like the price you paid for them. Get rid of excess stuff by all means (especially if you are looking at more than a 20ft container load!)

Finally, although it is undeniably expensive; very few people regret taking the chance. Even of the people who choose to head back and not stay out here permanently: very few regret giving it a go. It is almost unheard of that people make the move and don't get a huge amount out of doing it. For some it may be that they found the UK really was where they wanted to be. They still had a life changing experience and don't regret it.

HOW ON EARTH DO WE GET STARTED?

Never Surrender Dreams
J. Michael Straczynski

"That's a tall order."
"Perhaps. But where is it written that all our dreams must be small ones?"
Babylon 5:"No Compromises"
J. Michael Straczynski

So, you just got off the plane and you are starting this wonderful new life. Once you have slept a wee bit, grabbed a reviving cup of coffee or two and paddled at the beach, get budgeting.

Yeah right! As they say here.

Actually as odd as it may seem, if you are still in the UK when you are reading this then my advice is to start getting your finances under control now. I feel that the **number one best decision** I made before coming here (other than to actually come here of course) was to get my finances sorted and stop wasting money. You really don't need to wait till you are in New Zealand to get that "non-consumerist" lifestyle.

If you are after a simple life, I think you will find it a bit easier to get one here than in the UK. But I have to say that if you were to make the same decisions in the UK you would probably be able to live a pretty simple life there too. (Ok, more people may look at you as though you've sprouted horns 😀).

If you start now as you mean to live here, firstly it won't come as a shock to the system, and as a bonus, you will have more money to start your new life with! I think that being able to come over here without the UK debt hanging over us gave us a huge sense of freedom. And it meant that the proceeds from our house sale were wholly available to get us started, buy a house (and in our case splash out on a completely consumerist, and utterly guilt free 42" Plasma TV. I may not spend often – but when I do – I like to make it count! 😊).

I've never exactly followed the rules so it was relatively easy for me to make the decision to live a little differently in the UK and stop spending. To be perfectly honest, it's often the same here as well. There are quite a few people in New Zealand who do splash their money on designer clothes, flash cars and expensive TV's (😊). Some people can afford them; many can't and put it on plastic or Hire Purchase.

The thing is: whatever country you live in – you don't have to follow the crowd. Who the hell wants to keep up with the Joneses anyway? The Joneses are usually broke! (No offence if you happen to be Mr. or Mrs. Jones!) Many people still cannot accept that I do not need to look for a job; either for the money, or because I need something to do. And it still boggles the minds of most people that by me not working, we are in fact better off than when we both worked. I've always found that if you choose not to follow the crowd, there will always be people who look at you a bit funny, and judge you. I have a sort of "who cares" attitude to that, but if you are not used to it, it can be a bit hard to deal with. Bear this in mind when you start taking care of your money. Most people do not do this, and think it very strange when other people do!

I **know** how hard it is to turn your financial life around. I've done it. Twice. Some people understand money and finances really easily, but if you are not one of those people – then please be assured that I'm not either. None of this has come easily to me. It's been a struggle to understand where to put my money, how to pay off a mortgage (even to realise that I **could** pay a mortgage off in under 25 years). And the thought of investing used to bring me out in cold sweats. Even now, taxes have a disturbing tendency to turn my brain to jelly 😨).

We started out with over £14,000 worth of credit card debt and overdrafts. That was on top of a £140,000 mortgage. We were hemorrhaging money and in a right old pickle.

Now – we have no debt other than the mortgage ($157,000 now £62,800 at the original exchange rate of 2.5). We have an emergency fund of about $15k just in case, and other savings of a few thousand for things on the house. We own shares, and currently own 3 rental properties (which are not in such a state that I wouldn't let other human beings live in them😊.) We've realised that we don't just have to settle for "Doing OK"; that we can – If we work at it – do rather well. We didn't get this far by being lucky. We did it by learning **how** to do it – and then **doing it**.

But you know what – the only way to get there – is to **start**.

I really recommend that you get yourself over to the Emigratenz forum (www.emigratenz.org/forum) and introduce yourself. This is by far the best of the Internet forums that I have been on, and while there is still the odd bit of argy bargy on there, it is a whole lot more friendly and polite that a lot of other forums. This is where to go to get help and encouragement from people who are on the same journey as you. You will meet people at the same stage as you, and people who have been settled in New Zealand for years. You will see people who love it here, and people who hate it here and can't wait to get back. You can get help, encouragement, and sometimes – just people who will listen to you venting your frustrations with the whole process. Most importantly – you will make friends.

Living in New Zealand is just amazing. I only have to look out of my windows and see the mountains in the distance – and I have to pinch myself to make sure I'm not dreaming. This is an amazing journey you are about to set out on, and I hope you enjoy it every step of the way. It's not always an easy journey – there can be many days when the stress of trying to emigrate just gets too much. There are days once you get here where the homesickness is almost unbearable, and more than one person I know (including me) has wanted nothing more than to get on the next plane out of here. But for each of us that arrives here – the journey will always be different. New Zealand is not for everyone, and some people will go home. There's nothing wrong with that.

It is okay not to like everything about New Zealand once you get here. It is okay to have doubts about whether or not this is the place for you and your family. It is okay to struggle with adapting to your new life. It is okay to miss your old life and family. It is even okay to miss the UK. These things do not make you an unsuccessful migrant, and these things certainly do not mean that you should bugger off back where you came from.

Just remember that no matter what you do or where you end up – it's your life, and it's your choice. If you get that visa, and get on that plane, you are living the life that most people only dream of – and never dare to live.

> *There is no "one true path" to emigrating.*
> *Avalon.*

RECOMMENDED BOOKS AND WEBSITES

Avalon's Guide
www.avalonsguide.com
For updates: the problem with a book that relies on tax policy, immigration rules, and interest rates – is that they change so often. So visit the website to see what changes are occurring and any news that I think migrants could do with knowing about finances.

You will also find downloads of the budget sheets you can use, and you can contact me through the website for help if you need to.

Your Mortgage and how to pay it off in five years
Your Mortgage and How to Save $50,000 to $250,000 per Property
Your Money; Starting out and starting over
Anita Bell

Please note that Your Mortgage now has a new Subtitle so you will probably see it for sale as: Your Mortgage and How to Save $50,000 to $250,000 per Property.

These are by far the best books I have read on anything to do with budgeting or money. They are funny, easy to read, and full of ridiculously good tips on surviving on a low wage and doing really well at it. It is these books that turned us from being in a right mess – to being quite comfy. I cannot recommend them enough – I only wish I were on commission.

Unfortunately this book does not seem to be available in the UK. Although it is written for New Zealand so much of the facts and figures don't relate to the UK – the basis and ideas are amazing. So if you come here on a trip – grab one! Grab 10 and give them your mates!

The Courage to Be Rich
Suze Orman
It's a bit "oddball" in places, but does take you though some very good and sound money saving principles. A good background book to help get you thinking a different way rather than a "how to" book. Also, it's targeted to a US audience so some of the info just isn't relevant to here or the UK.

The Money Diet
Martin Lewis
www.moneysavingexpert.com
A UK book. He is brilliant, great sense of humour and a real champion against overcharging (especially by the banks). Website – you can get weekly emails with money saving ideas – but it's only useful for the UK. Also has a great forum on there where you can get loads of ideas and help. Especially useful if you have problem debts. I think everyone who is serious about budgeting and debt reduction should head over there.

Don't Sign Anything!
Neil Jenman
www.jenman.com.au
The book to read before buying a house in New Zealand – especially at Auction.

Rich Dad Poor Dad
Robert Kiyosaki
A whole series of books – but start with the title one. These are American books – so lots of stuff not relevant to New Zealand or the UK as such – but good principles. If you want to do

more than budget and save – these are good books to help you on the way to investing. Lots of information on Property Investing. Rich Dad believes that Financial Education is paramount. A lot of the later books are repetitive – but the first 4-6 are great.

Pay Zero Taxes
Slash Your taxes
Peter Sibbald
Deals with how to make the New Zealand tax system work for you by teaching you how to offset business or property costs against your personal income taxes. Neat!

Building Wealth Through Investment Property
Dolf De Roos
A kiwi now living rather well in the states and jet setting round the world speaking at seminars occasionally (I heard him recently – he's a great guy to listen to; literally bounces round the stage). This book was written in 1995 when interest rates were 15%+! A good book on the fundamentals – only talks about negative gearing though (which – on reflection is just right for today's market).

The Richest Man in Babylon
George S Clason
An old book – basically a parable about looking after money. It tells the story of a Babylonian Slave who becomes very wealthy – using a few simple rules such as "Set Thy Purse To fattening"! Love it.

The Millionaire Next Door
T Stanley & W Danko
If you think only bad people are rich, or you need to be lucky to be well off – this is the book that explodes the Myth. Interestingly – one of the things it states is that many millionaires get there because no matter what they earn –

someone takes care of the money, tracks and controls spending, takes care of the investing, and budgets. It also shows that high incomes are **not** necessary to become financially wealthy.

What Your Accountant Doesn't Tell You.
Fiona Clayton Law
Another New Zealand specific book, which takes you through some of the things you can do to increase your income or decrease your taxes legally in New Zealand.

Two Incomes and Still Broke.
Linda Kelly
I found this in Wellington City Library – and it was quite a find. As I've already said – we found by accident that we were better off once I gave up work, and started managing the finances. Well, this book actually takes you through the process of **why** you can often be worse off if you are a two-income family. It helps you work out how much extra you spend because you both work. It's a bit fiddly – but I really think it's worth doing – if only because most people struggle to believe that you can be better off on one income than you are on two.

The Two-Income Trap: Why Middle-Class Parents are Going Broke
Elizabeth Warren and Amelia Warren Tyagi
An eye-opening read. This book dispels a lot of myths about money, debt and why we need two incomes.

Debt Free, Ca$hed Up and Laughing
Cath Armstrong & Lee Anne Brighton
A small, nifty book about how to live frugally. Even has recipes for cleaning products, which while cheap, seem to rely on a lot of elbow grease. Also, the authors seem to feel you should always have things to do on hand in case of an

emergency five minutes where you could be wasting time relaxing! It does have a lot of good money saving tips though.
www.cheapskates.com.au

Maxed Out
James D Spurlock.
For those of you who are not yet suitably put-off by credit cards.

Sorted
www.sorted.org.nz
A sort of one-stop-shop for all things money in New Zealand (and hosted by a cute mouse!)

PropertyTalk
www.propertytalk.co.nz
For all things property investing – though you may need armour.

Richmastery
www.richmastery.co.nz
It's cheesy – but it's worth a look if you are thinking about investing in property.

Interest Rates
www.interest.co.nz
This website carries the latest interest rates in New Zealand, both for savings and borrowing.

Pension Transfers
www.uk-pension-transfer.co.nz
Talk to Alison about Pensions and Insurance. She is really very friendly, and very good at explaining what your options are.

A Good Mortgage Broker
Alan Borthwick at FSB4 and Mortgage Max
Email: alanb@fsb.co.nz
alan@mortgagemax.co.nz

Web: www.fsb.co.nz
www.mortgagemax.co.nz

In fact – he's so good – he may just be getting me to set up a Kiwisaver account! If you need specific advice about what to do with your money, beyond budgeting and not spending it – give Alan a call. He is also an active investor – so he puts his money where his mouth is.

Crown Relocations
www.crownrelo.com

The Inland Revenue
www.ird.govt.nz

Money Saving Expert
www.moneysavingexpert.com
Home of a pretty spectacular array of money saving tools and forums.

Compound Interest Calculator
www.moneychimp.com/calculator/compound_interest_calculator.htm
Just in case you ever want to see how compound interest really does make your saving grow.

Mortgage Calculator
www.westpac.co.nz
Use the "Fine Tune Your Loan" calculator for comparing different loans.

Meeting other migrants.
www.emigratenz.org/forum

Moving your Money
www.hifx.co.nz or www.hifx.co.uk

For good rental properties in Wellington
www.propertyman.co.nz
This is the company I use to manage my Wellington rentals. They provide a fantastic service for both tenants and landlords. They look after me, but most importantly, they look after my tenants, so that they don't get hacked off and leave.